For
Brigid and Margaret O'Connor

Crowds of miserable Irish darken all our towns. The wild Milesian features, looking false ingenuity, restlessness, unreason, misery, and mockery salute you on all highways and byways—in his rags and laughing savagery . . . [the Irishman] is there to undertake all work that can be done by mere strength of hand and back.

—THOMAS CARLYLE, *Chartism*, 1842

The Irish in Britain live miraculously normal lives in the very difficult circumstances of fitting themselves into a strange environment.

—PEADER O'DONNELL,
Commission on Emigration and Population Problems,
Dublin, 1954

I feel resentful of drunken Irish labour in our streets, of the incredible Irish labour racket operating in favour of the Irish on our building projects, and of the enormous tax-free British cheques cashed at that special Irish pub on Friday.

—Extract from letter to the *Irish Times*,
December 1971, from an English reader

Contents

Acknowledgements

Apart from the miscellaneous reading matter later credited, the author is indebted to:

Hutchinson & Co., London, for permission to quote from *Borstal Boy*, by Brendan Behan (1958); *The Railway Navvies* by Terry Coleman (1965).

McGibbon & Kee, London, for permission to quote from *With Breast Expanded* by Brian Behan, 1964.

Martin, Brian, and O'Keefe for the quotation from *The Green Fool*, by Patrick Kavanagh, London, 1971.

Elspeth Kyle and the Camberwell Council on Alcoholism for the interview on pp. 129–35.

Mr Patrick Mulloy, London, for use of the postcard from Bernard Shaw, quoted on pp. 60–1.

Runnymede Industrial Unit, London, and author Shelley Markham, for quotations from the pamphlet *'What About the Irish?'* (1971).

The library staffs of the British Museum; Catholic Central Library, London; the Institute of Race Relations, London; The Irish Club, and Irish Embassy, London.

A debt is also owed to Noel O'Connell, who provided able direction in researching the post-Famine settlements and to Marie McGibbon (née Brock) whose original thesis on the aftermath of one such settlement – the Stockport Riots – was invaluable.

For insight into conditions in the building industry of the 1930s, I am indebted to the recently deceased Dominic Donnelly and for first-hand accounts of strikes in that same industry in the fifties, I am grateful to Brian Behan, Jack Henry, John Palmer, Pat O'Donovan.

Many people helped me in examining 'social problems' among the present-day Irish, including Maura Dorgan, C. D. Hunt, Fathers Sheridan and O'Donnell; others, who wish to remain anonymous, were equally informative. Further specialized knowledge of the Irish was provided by James Cantwell, James Kirby, Richard Kershaw, Paul Dwyer, Henry Harris.

Able research assistance was provided by Carol Lazebrey, Margaret O'Connor, William Pinching, Jillian Orr. All are of course absolved from any conclusions which may appear contentious, but I cannot absolve them from their generous assistance in making the work possible.

KEVIN O'CONNOR
London, 1972

PART I

HISTORICAL BACKGROUND

Before 1800

The first trickle which was to become the stream of Irish immigration to Britain can be traced to the twelfth-century Anglo-Norman invasion of Ireland, when Henry II conveniently directed some energetic barons to annex the neighbouring island. The Irish tribal chiefs, more interested in cousinly squabbles, were easy meat for the mailed and armoured Normans; many of the dispossessed Irish set off to settle in the more populous English towns; England, then as now, being no more than a fair day's sail away at the narrowest points of the channel.

England had a more developed social structure in the towns and here the Irish refugees lost themselves. Some, with perhaps the beginning of what the native Englishman still sees as Irish cunning and blarney, ingratiated themselves into the Saxon community as street vendors and labourers. The majority, lacking guile and easily discernible as foreign, existed among the riff-raff that seeks warmth and food in any town, to the extent that in 1243 a statute was invoked for the expulsion of Irish beggars, which had the bizarre side-effect of driving the more able into service in the feudal armies. Thus, perhaps, was initiated the tradition of Irish service in the army of the conqueror.

The Irish continued to come across St George's Channel in regular shipments, 'footloose and weary', and to scavenge in the homeland of those who had driven them out of their own hearths. The influx was given a fresh boost by the relentless warfare in Ireland in the sixteenth and seventeenth centuries. Speaking a different language and coming from a less regimented if besieged tribal society, the majority of immigrants again sought solace in the lower echelons of the host society. And so, four hundred years after the enactment of the first law to expel Irish beggars, a similar one was passed in 1629, except this time they were called vagrants!

Thus, during the four hundred years between the thirteenth

a..d seventeenth century, the image was formalized of the Irish as slovenly intruders upon the green and pleasant land of England. There were exceptions—Irishmen operated successfully as merchants in the English ports. Even after the disintegration of the feudal structure, resulting in the sharp division of English society, between 'gentlemen' and others, there were individuals of talent and daring (like the playwright Sheridan) who successfully assailed the social, literary, and political heights of their adopted country.

For most of the Irish, however, the towns offered merely drudgery and refuge—and not only to the Irish, but also the native English cast off from a depressed rural economy. The Irish were easily distinguished by their accents, appearances, habits, and all those traits of character which constitute the 'stage Irishman', who now emerged as a phenomenon of the English urban scene. One of the first 'stage Irishmen' appeared in a play produced in London in 1761:

> I'm at the Harp and Spinning Wheel,
> in Farthing-Fields, Wapping
> In a room of my own, I hire at ninepence
> A week.

If that Irish stage character was based on one who had indeed a room of his own, then he was fortunate. Most of his compatriots had more cramped accommodation. As for his rent of ninepence a week, it was no more than a gentleman would pay for a meal of ten dishes. The Irish character proved popular with audiences, which is more than can be recorded for the real-life models who formed a furtive influx. Competition for work led to riots between Irish and native labourers, and after such fracas the unlucky injured were charged and sentenced, often to deportation. Some of the Irish found themselves transported in chains to the colonies, and it was poor consolation to know they were helping initiate the worldwide diaspora of their race. If was also of small consolation to know that some of their more business-minded compatriots in the ports earned a hefty living from transportation, the going-rate being in the region of £1,000 per hundred men-inmanacles. They also encountered sporadic sectarian animosity, of which the most famous eighteenth-century manifestations were the anti-Catholic Gordon Riots of 1780.

Nevertheless, most survived riots, enmity, and the playwright's flourish. In spite of the existence of religious antagonism, the parliamentary concessions to Roman Catholics (in England and Ireland alike) which had begun in the 1770s were continued, and in 1792 the Irish opened their first semi-public Church, St Patrick's, in London. By 1790 they had become established in the ghettos of the major ports of London, Bristol, and Liverpool. In that latter city, in 1790, there were 7,000 cellar dwellings—rank, humid, and insanitary—but ready to take the teeming Irish who trekked off the boats from Dublin stunned and sick from the twelve-hour, open-deck crossing.

By 1880 emigration to Britain had become a tradition. It is easy to see the reasons for this. Nine-tenths of Ireland's population was dependent upon agriculture; and the evils of the tenurial system, with its dues, rack-rents, evictions, combined with bad harvests and the repressive policies of the government, made life for the depressed and demoralized peasantry grossly insecure. The extraordinary population boom which began in the latter part of the eighteenth century led to uneconomic subdivisions of farms as more and more people tried to eke out a precarious living from insufficient resources. In such circumstances emigration was bound to remain a persistent feature of Irish rural life, while its effects on English urban life were to become increasingly noticeable.

1800–1845

Under the Act of Union of 1800 Ireland ceased to be a separate state and was merged with Great Britain to form the United Kingdom. This measure was achieved by the wholesale corruption of the Irish parliament and with the connivance of the Catholic Church in Ireland and England. Because their loyalty was suspect, Catholic leaders were intensely wary of offending the Government in the period of uneasily developing relations following their partial restoration to civil rights, and were only too glad to support its Irish policy. Among those who canvassed for the Union were bishops in Ireland and Irish priests in Britain.

The Union had disastrous and far-reaching economic, social, and political consequences. In rural Ireland, particularly, conditions deteriorated drastically. The number of absentee landlords rose sharply; gross mismanagement of estates prevailed; and the constant demand for higher rents meant that the country's agricultural produce was sold, mainly for export, in order to provide payment for meagre land holdings. The ever-growing cottier class was thus reduced to the level of subsisting on the potato, and in years of shortage their plight was desperate and the rate of emigration correspondingly high.

In the first half of the nineteenth century the number of Irish immigrants in Britain was sufficiently great to constitute a social problem. In 1840 Thomas Carlyle wrote: 'The time has come when the Irish population must either be improved a little, or else exterminated.' The size and cohesion of immigrant communities was sufficient to necessitate some degree of acceptance from the native population, an acceptance punctuated by outbursts of hostility, generally taking the form of attacks upon the Irish ghetto areas in the large cities, vicious battles between rival work gangs, and agricultural disturbances. These and other expressions of communal antagonism were almost always occasioned by a combination of factors in the eyes of the natives: the Irish were strike-breakers who would gladly work for a lower wage; their religion was an alien one; they were dirty, disease-ridden, unkempt, drunken, fractious, and separate.

The fiercest clashes between the Irish immigrants and the native working class took place in Scotland. Here the bitterness was intensified by clear-cut religious differences. Irish Protestants, particularly those from the northern counties, were welcomed by the Scots, but the Irish Catholics were abused, while their churches were ransacked and their cabins wrecked and burned.

The motivation for such attacks was not fundamentally theological, but rather the resentment which any indigenous human society expresses towards the presence of an 'alien' body with which it feels threatened. That the indigenous society should feel thus threatened points to an underlying economic reaction. It was the misfortune of the Irish—no strangers themselves to resisting alien presence on their native soil—that the Britain they came to in the 1830s and 1840s was one of already simmering unrest, due mainly to the dislocative effects of the Industrial Revolution, which threatened the welfare of an agriculturally based proletariat. The English and Scots saw the Irish immigrants as an intrusive element within an essentially British social structure and treated them accordingly.

This last fact alone is sufficient indication that already the Union had failed. The refugee Irish of the early nineteenth century could hold the Act of Union largely responsible for the wretched standard of living from which they had fled. And to some of the more politically perceptive of them it might have seemed as if that act had made manifestly evil their present state. At its door they could bitterly lay their condition of poverty, deprivation, and hostility to their religion. Had they been less nationalistically insular they would have noted that the lot of the native English working classes was little better, that in fact both communities were equally victims of the class-cum-capital structure of the nineteenth century, and that both were about to be steamrolled under the weight of the advancing Industrial Revolution. Instead, with their penchant for self-pity and hindsight, the Irish immigrants saw only the rural stretches of that land from which they had been driven by famine, by unscrupulous land agents and by the Act of Union.

Even if the Irish Catholic community in Britain had formed an integrated body of political opinion, they could not turn to the natural leaders of the community—the clergy—for the political guidance they needed. The Roman Church was still feeling its way cautiously and uncertainly in its relations with the Government; and although the Irish immigrants were rapidly outnumbering the fifty thousand English Catholics, the real power in that Church was held by the scions of the old English families.

When Roman Catholic opinion eventually asserted itself, it

was as an essentially Irish movement under Irish leadership and relying for its active support on the submerged masses of the Irish countryside. Daniel O'Connell's successful campaign for Catholic Emancipation, as a result of which Roman Catholics were at last admitted to the House of Commons, removed the most important remaining stigma against their religion. More significant from the point of view of Irishmen, whether in Britain or the home country, was the fact that the victory of the 'Liberator' freed them psychologically from their own communal weight of inadequacy.

If their new-found identity gave them moral strength, it also had its disadvantages. It fortified their sense of narrow penitential nationalism and encouraged them in their resistance to anti-Irish, anti-Catholic discrimination. In Britain, by extension, this engendered renewed fears on the part of the native inhabitants and greatly increased hostility against the Irish communities. The very physical import of throngs of Irish labourers crowding the new and restored churches must have been seen in terms of a political power-base with resultant flutterings of unease among a government coping with various fronts of potential disturbance—in the rural areas with agitation for higher wages, in the cities with pressure for electoral reform, and in Ireland with the periodic sparks to the power-key of nationalism.

O'Connell's radicalism, such as it was, did not extend to improving the conditions of life and work of the Irish peasantry, and certainly not the dispossessed peasantry floundering in the midst of the British Industrial Revolution. His other great objective, once Emancipation had been secured, was the Repeal of the Union. But Repeal was not to be achieved until generations after O'Connell's death. There is little evidence to show that Repeal would have improved the lot of the immigrants, unless with the optimism of despair they assumed that a restored Irish parliament would have shipped them all back to the fondly imagined green and pleasant pastures.

Nevertheless, O'Connell's activity was the earliest radical influence upon the Irish in Britain. Far more radical was the influence of another movement which was contemporary with O'Connell's career as a Westminster M.P. This was Chartism,

which sought to unite and organize *all* elements of the working classes in Britain in order to eradicate the feudal-capitalistic
basis of society. Many Irish immigrants were closely involved
with the movement and its principal leader was Feargus
O'Connor, who sat in parliament as M.P. for Cork. O'Connor
was originally a protégé of O'Connell, but their collaboration
broke on a mixture of personal spleen and differing political
philosophies. O'Connor had effective sympathy with the
labouring class. O'Connell had little. O'Connor wanted to unite
Irish and English workers for their joint betterment. O'Connell, a landowner, feared the organization of the proletariat.
While O'Connell played on the immigrants' nostalgia for an
independent Catholic Ireland, O'Connor campaigned for their
well-being in Britain, for the alleviation of their condition in
the slums and sweat-shops of the Industrial Revolution. The
divergence between these two attitudes was so extreme that on
occasions O'Connell's supporters broke up Chartist meetings
and serious fighting ensued. For years, therefore, the Irish
community itself was splintered, thus reducing its potential
of becoming a viable political influence.

O'Connell's ideas ultimately won the day: Chartism petered
out after 1848. Yet O'Connor's message was not forgotten,
and his demands continued to be urged in nineteenth- and
twentieth-century Britain, and many of them were eventually
realized in the formation of trade unions, universal adult suf-
frage, the reduction of upper-class power, the provision of
civil rights for deprived sections of the community, and the
general improvement of social conditions. Like their British
counterparts, the immigrant Irish workers benefited from
these gradually advancing improvements, not because they
were Irish but because they belonged to the lowest stratum
of *British* society.

However, this is a very long-term view of developments.
For the Irish in Britain during the 'hungry forties' life was
still extremely difficult. Their living conditions were appalling,
their work hard and badly paid, and discriminations and
violence against them rife.

Meanwhile in the home-country, party politics and reform
movements had little relevance to the condition of the major-

ity of the inhabitants, who were concerned solely with staying alive and raising enough money to pay rents. The general standard of living was far worse than it had been at any earlier time and was deteriorating still further as the soaring birth-rate led to the inevitable presence of more people than could properly be accommodated in the existing economic environment. In 1845 over four million—more than half the total population—were relying for their entire subsistence on a single vegetable, the potato. The situation was one of immense potential danger.

THE FAMINE EMIGRATION 1846–1852

During the period 1845–8 the potato crop failed completely and one million Irish died of disease and starvation. Emigration received a panic impetus, and in the hysterical rush to escape from the doomed island over a million sickly, impoverished peasants put to sea. The massive exodus continued at the rate of 200,000 a year between 1849 and 1852. Half of these came to Britain: they could afford no more than the cross-channel fare of threepence. Through the port of Liverpool in one year passed three hundred thousand ravaged Irish; to Glasgow journeyed fifty thousand; to Manchester went twenty thousand; to London two hundred and fifty thousand. On arrival, the demoralized escapees ran the gauntlet of abuse from dockers as they disembarked from ships widely held to be disease-carriers. They were so cowed, suspicious, and superstitious that they created instant ghettos in their areas of settlement. A year after the Famine struck, and while it still raged in Ireland, the British cities of Manchester, Glasgow, and London had all sprouted their 'Little Irelands'.

Today, one hundred and thirty years after the Famine diaspora, the districts thus settled are still identified as Irish: Hammersmith, Camden Town, Paddington, and Islington in London; the Gorbals in Glasgow; Stockport, and the Newtown areas of Manchester and Cardiff; Scotland Road in Liverpool. From the entry port of Liverpool they joined the road from Holyhead, heading for London. The influences of that trek are apparent today, in that on or near the route, the

Great North Road, were the growing towns of Wolverhampton, Coventry, and Luton, towns which today hold strong Irish contingents. And where the Great North Road came into London was the then pleasant and leafy village of Camden. (So much for the popular legend which ascribes Camden Town's Irishness to being as far from Euston Station as an Irishman can travel carrying two suitcases on a Friday night!)

Eastward from the port of Bristol came the Great West Road and along this route was the town of Reading and further in towards London the village of Hammersmith, and in both of these areas the fearful, fleeing Irish settled. They came, too, into the Port of London and into the district of Rosemary Lane in the East End which soon came to be known as 'Little Ireland'. The areas in which they settled were, for the most part, the decaying districts of the towns and cities festering with latent fever. Contemporary accounts are colourful and unflattering: 'The Irish were crowded together with all their native habits of filth and indolence,' wrote the author of a fever report.

Yet it was an alien body of growing substance and impact. The Irish were increasingly represented at all labouring levels of English society: in the factories and ports, in the harvest fields of Scotland, in the collieries of Wales and further south to the farms of Kent, and beyond to Devon and Cornwall. In the growing towns they were increasingly becoming the leg-up of the rising bourgeoisie, as domestic servants and maids. A contemporary account of one such classic Irish maidservant poignantly perceives the quality of separateness, and not least the differences of language and culture. The incident was recounted by a distressed gentlewoman to that social reporter, Mayhew.

... and if the Irish hussy didn't spill a whole basinful of water on the floor, and then actually seemed in no way inclined to wipe up the slop on the boards. So I begged she should take a cloth and do it immediately. But the minx replied: 'Oh, sure and don't it always soak in, in my country.' Which was a good deal more than I felt I ought to put up with. So I told her very plainly, 'that her country ... must be a filthy, dirty place and only fit for pigs to wallow in.' No sooner were the words out of my mouth, than she turned round sharp upon me, and shrieking out 'Hoo! Hubbaboo!' seized the kitchen carving knife and brandishing it over her head cried out, 'Hurrah for ould Ireland, the first jim of the say—and a yard of cowld steel for them as spakes agin' her!'

The media of the times are littered with such accounts of the feckless, fey, fighting Irish. Reporters in search of 'human interest' stories crowded the courts when cases involving Irish were heard, for they could be sure of choice actions and phraseology with which to regale their readers. Male defendants were invariably described as a broth of a boy, as fine a sprig as ever flourished in the Ould Emerald Isle, or introduced along lines of: Big Blarney, Bould Mike, Poor Paddy.

This was the newspaper equivalent of the music-hall compounded in equal parts of affection, fear, and racial superiority. Certainly the living conditions of the Irish—at the bottom of the pile—allied to their growing numbers provided ample material for the courts. By 1861, *one quarter* of the population of Liverpool was Irish-born, yet Irish names accounted for *over half* the offences of assault, attack, inebriation, disturbance of the peace. By 1871, over 800,000 Irish-born lived in the 'Little Irelands' of Britain, and most of these ghettos were shunned by 'respectable' citizens and the police entered only in numbers.

Thus did the Irish put down their weak, grudging roots into the insanitary slums of the Industrial Revolution. In a way the timing of the Industrial Revolution was fortunate for the Irish. It allowed them the full rein of energy and work, and its circumstances dictated some element of common toil with the native population. The new mills for cotton, coal, and iron and steel were hungry for human fodder. The English workers came reluctantly from the countryside and found their new life as strange as did the Irish. The irony was that at the same time as Ireland's back was broken by the Great Famine and its despoliation of people, England was on the brink of riches beyond the dreams of even the most avaricious fledgling capitalist. In the mid-nineteenth century England was the greatest industrial nation in the world. Half the world's coal was raised from her pits; half the world's textiles came from Lancashire mills; one third of the world's output of manufactured goods travelled in British ships.

The key to this booming wealth was the evolution of mechanical ability—the means whereby iron and steel could be fashioned, which in turn developed the methods to extract it in massive quantities from the hitherto harbouring earth. Impetus begat impetus with the steam locomotive spanning iron bridges to traverse the country to reach expanding ports, where larger steam-driven ships ferried the export goods to the captive markets of the colonies.

The great iron and steel revolution was, however, conducted on gross human inequalities. The general demeaning conditions of the labouring populace, the child-labour and the short wretched life-span of the working classes have been sufficiently well documented. This was the contemporary urban grimness to which the famine-fleeing Irish came, hoping for little more than the means of survival. It was only to be expected that the natives would react with vehemence to the sickly hordes who came teeming among them. Their bitter resentment was further exacerbated in this period of strongly, even militantly held, Protestantism by the fact that the Irish belonged to the feared and hated Church of Rome. Acts of violence against the Irish communities therefore became more frequent during the late 1840s and in Scotland sometimes reached the alarming proportions of full-scale civil disturbance.

In such circumstances it is hardly surprising that the congested Irish ghettos developed as tight, clannish communities whose residents retained a distinctive identity and some semblance of their national culture. They spoke Irish, dressed in black waistcoats, cloaks, and shawls, brewed drink, smoked pipes, and fought with sticks—all marks of savagery to the British natives on the outside. They also clung tenaciously to their nourished version of the Church of Rome, their defined nationalism made them suspicious of English priests and they preferred to be guided, in temporal as well as spiritual matters,

by their own Irish priests, whom they regarded as their natural
tribal leaders.

The defiant Catholicism of the Famine refugees was to complete the process of revitalizing the Roman Catholic Church
in England. By 1852 the British convert and intellectual, John
Henry Newman, was able to declare: 'The English Church
was not, and the English Church is once again ... It is the
coming of the Second Spring.' Numerous Catholic historians
have even seen in the ravages of famine nothing less than the
hand of providence in bringing about this 'Second Spring' and
restoring the Catholic faith to England.

1850–1900

The Industrial Revolution provided work and livelihood for
the new arrivals. In the ripening coalfields of Wales, in the
cotton-mills of Manchester, in the ports of London and of
Liverpool they worked fiercely, furtively, and with the urgent
awareness that work, in its most critical sense, meant survival.
Most dramatic, perhaps, was their contribution to the railways, which were so vital in opening up new dimensions of
territory and transport.

In a sense the railways and the Industrial Revolution begat
each other. During the nineteenth century 20,000 miles of
railway passage were dug, hewed, and blasted across England,
immense undertakings of engineering skill and navvy labour,

> And drill, ye terriers drill
> Drill, ye terriers, drill
> It's work all day for sugar in your tay
> Down beyond the railway.

By the middle of the century the navvies had evolved the
skilled toughness of intent and behaviour which was to lend
them a special glamour and reputation, separate from that of
general labourers.

The Irish navvies had to be content with the resentment
of the native navvies: for all the handed-down myths that the
Irish built the railways, rarely did they exceed 30 per cent

of the overall labour force. Antipathy against them was strong, and pitched battles occurred between navvy groups of opposing nationalities. The English navvy was a craftsman and often a countryman who took immense pride in his calling, fancying himself as something of an engineer (which he often needed to be) and bitterly resented the unskilled Irish intruder. In the words of a ballad:

> When work grew scarce and bread was dear
> and wages lessened too,
> the Irish hordes were bidders here
> our half-paid work to do.

The most vicious hostility, as always, came from the groups of Scottish workmen who, with pick-handles at the ready, trampled across the country to flay the Irish, burn their huts, and terrorize their women. After one such expedition, the *Scottish Herald* reported that:

> It was truly pitiable to see several of the wives of the Irish labourers sitting, at short distance from the blazing huts, in the midst of a few articles of furniture which they were able to save from the flames, wrapped up in the cloaks peculiar to their country, and watching with melancholy countenances the gradual demolition of their humble dwellings.

As a result of regular attacks of this type, Irish navvies never worked alongside the Scots and only rarely with the English. The only recorded instance of harmony between the Irish and the native workmen appears to have been with the Cornish and Devon miners with whom they were engaged in tunnel blasting on the Midland railways in 1870.

But if the Irish endured much, they also occasionally retaliated when favoured by superior numbers; and the railway work at least uprooted some of them from the more decayed ghettos and led them to find new ones of marginally improved comfort. Its more significant effect was to involve them more fully in the general labour market of which the pick-and-shovel navvies were the princes. It was the first communal involvement of the diasporic Irish to the expanding land of their adoption.

An examination of how the Irish were assimilated to the East End of London, by then the melting-pot of immigration, is instructive. Here the Irish developed two earned identities of some respect, those of tunnel diggers and street vendors. The men worked in the near-by docks which were being furiously expanded to cope with the outpouring exports of the Industrial Revolution, while their wives and children sold trinkets and fruit from barrows in the streets. Even with such dramatic expansion of the ports, work in the East End was not regularly plentiful, and for those who had to idle the day out, the street selling of their families made the vital difference.

Street trading brought the Irish into contact with that other great diasporic nation, the Jews, against whom they found themselves competing for an economic foothold. By their qualities of persistence and toughness they managed to wean the monopoly of street trading away from the Jews. Mayhew noted:

> The Irish boy could live harder than the Jew—often in his own country he subsisted on a stolen turnip a day—he could lodge harder—lodge for a penny a night in any noisesome den, or sleep in the open air, which is seldom done by the Jew boy ... Thus, as the Munster or Connaught boy could live on less ... the Hebrew youths were displaced by the Irish in the street orange trade.

By the 1870s the East End had become sharply divided between Jewish and Irish districts. Mutual antagonism was intensified by later waves of Jewish exiles who, fleeing from the homicidal policies of Catholic monarchs in Europe, found their way blocked by Irish Catholics in Britain. In the event, the Jews won. Increasing waves of Jewish immigrants from Russia made inroads into 'Irish' territory and grafted back most of the street trade.

By the end of the century the London Irish had become established and accepted, albeit with an air of separateness about their settlement. The music-halls and newspapers exhibited the most obvious manifestations of this growing acceptance. The 'stage Irish' character, exploiting the national penchant for colourful turns of phrase, the fey response to questioning and the self-mocking seriousness (all marks of a defensive people) provided ideal material for music-hall jokes, while journalists reporting court cases involving Irishmen could always be sure of choice actions and phraseology with which to regale their readers. The stage Irishman was at the height of his popularity at the end of the nineteenth century, and for all its ingratiating idiocy and bogus sentimentality, such folk hero status was welcomed by the mass of the Irish. In spite of the criticisms of later generations of immigrants in less dangerous times, their reasoning was sound: the caricature and ridicule meant that the English considered them harmless creatures. In the East End of the nineteenth century, regularly hovering on the brink of racial conflict, this refusal to take them seriously ensured their safety and marked the thin end of the wedge towards general acceptance.

If the Irish of the East End were thus agreeable to being exalted on the stage, their counterparts in other areas of the country were often less flexible. In the textile mills of the Midlands the Irish became prominent in affairs of industrial agitation and were quick to participate in labour disputes. The lists of those arrested after such agitation frequently contain a disproportionate number of Irish names. So while in London the quality of 'separateness' had been chronicled on the stage, in the Midlands the same separateness was recorded in the industrial agitation of the times. Add to these characteristics the obvious Irish influence on the growth of Roman Catholicism in England and one has the defining characteristics of an alien body in a host society.

The grudging acceptance they were accorded by the end of the nineteenth century was partly due to this very quality of 'separateness'. Unfortunately the convenient mythology of identity so mutually conspired to in this period survives today at various levels of English life—including Government—and is one of the most sinister legacies of the Famine diaspora.

But in the immediate post-Famine period the ordinary

English urban workers found it impossible to foster charitable notions regarding the throngs of Irish destitutes who descended in ever-increasing quantities into their midst, who upset the balance of labour by undercutting their meagre wages, and who, as soon as they could afford it, sent cash remittances home so that their families might join them. Their alien religion and their hostile views only served to aggravate the apparent menace. The high point of such antagonism was reached with the Stockport Riots of 1852, which compounded the elements of economic fear, racial hostility, and religious hysteria among an already intimidated population. The political prompt to the disorder was the re-establishment from Rome of the Catholic Hierarchy in Britain in 1850, wherein, in the decree of Pope Pius IX, the Church 'may again flourish in the Kingdom of England'.

The move was reacted to with alarm by the Government who passed the Ecclesiastical Titles Bill. Among other preventions, the Bill forbade the carrying of Catholic insignia and banners in public places, resulting in bitterness among Catholics. The Irish Catholics, already defiant and resentful in religion by the ferocity of penal repression in Ireland, were put in a defensive mood. Stockport, an outlying town of Manchester, provided the flashpoint. In the county of Lancashire of the 1850s lived almost a quarter of the immigrant Irish population of Britain, drawn there by the weaving and spinning employment of the cotton mills. The town of Stockport held a strong Irish ghetto which had grown from a mere 300 at the beginning of the century to over 8,000 by 1852. They were, by contemporary accounts, an unruly community in a state of tense antagonism with the native English workers. Existing in overcrowded, crumbling houses, along Rock Row and Bridge Street, the Irish were 'likely to turn out at a moment's notice and set on the first person they met and maltreat him cruelly'.

Thus the Irish of Stockport, surly and quick to take offence: their impending annual procession in June 1852, coming some days after the Royal Proclamation of the Ecclesiastical Titles Bill, saw opposing forces ranged. The following account captures the atmosphere and sequence of what ensued:

The Royal Proclamation had been hailed as a sectarian triumph by the lower classes and they had boasted that they would see the proclamation enforced in the case of the 'red-necked scholars', as they termed the Roman Catholic children.

The Irish decided that the annual meeting of scholars was not a procession of the sort prohibited and published their resolve to make their demonstration as usual. There was great excitement on the subject and it was said that the authorities thought of preventing the school gathering; but when the day came, the Protestants seemed less excited and the schools were allowed to make their procession without interruption. The Sunday passed off without disturbance, a fact which may have been due to the presence of a body of strong Irishmen who accompanied the procession, which studiously avoided any R.C. insignia.

The whole incident appeared to be closed when on the following day many personal encounters began to take place between Irish and English parties originating from a disturbance in a beerhouse. On Tuesday there were still more evident signs of commotion and some street fights occurred during which the windows of St Peter's school (Protestant) were broken. This led to a general mêlée in St Peter's Square when some stones were thrown through the windows of Alderman Graham's house. Rioting then became general and serious; so fierce in fact that the police could not suppress it. The rioting lasted spasmodically for three days, being finally put down by dint of the combined efforts of the police who managed to hold the chief body of the rioters in check and of the mayor and magistrates who meanwhile had assembled and sworn in some hundreds of special constables. The civil power had just gained the upper hand when a body of military also turned out and the riots were quelled. In retaliation for the assault on St Peter's School by the Irish, the English had turned the fight into an attack on the houses and chapels of the Irish. The mob attacked an Irish-owned beerhouse, first demolishing the furniture and breaking the windows, finally attempting to set it on fire. They then proceeded to treat the houses on

Rock Row and down Bridge Street in like manner reducing them to complete wrecks. The mob next demolished Edgeley Chapel and the minister's house, nothing being left but the bare walls. The chapel of St Michael in King Street was then gutted; here also everything was destroyed. The list of seriously wounded comprised sixty-seven persons named; one man was killed and some others died of injuries received. Hundreds of Irish had fled from the town and slept in the fields for weeks, fearing to return to their homes lest there should be a renewal of disturbances.[1]

Where religion was made the excuse for persecution of the Irish, it was predictable that their trenchant Catholicism would be reinforced. The Stockport Riots confirmed the immigrants in their sense of dual identity of being Irish *and* Catholic in Britain.

The greatly intensified rate of Irish emigration in the post-Famine years set a pattern which was to be maintained throughout the rest of the century.

The Irish slums were, as has been noted, invariably in the more decaying dilapidated districts of the cities. Street upon street of festering tenements; families living in single rooms, excrement piled in communal dumps in the ghettos; washing strung across cobbled or dirt streets; the whole overhung by insularity, insecurity, and deep suspicion of outsiders—these were the living conditions of the immigrants.

Within these self-contained, clannish communities men followed whatever trades they had learned in Ireland, though for the majority of them, having been drawn from the cottier class, there could be no such continuation and they had to adapt to labouring and navvying, to porterage and factoring. Some became dealers in fruit and vegetables; their names can still be seen on the store fronts of London's Covent Garden Market. Others developed entrepreneurial instincts as keepers of slum doss-houses and truck-shops (general and beer stores). The women, in respites from child-bearing, worked in factories and warehouses and the more artistic developed a flourishing

---

[1] Maire Brock, 'Irish Immigrants in Manchester, 1830–54', unpublished thesis, University of Southampton, 1962.

sideline in the manufacture of counterfeit coinage. Fighting was the most common law-breaking activity, generally occurring over inter-county rivalry, i.e. the Irish country of origin of any particular individual or group. The priests, by their academic training and by the nature of the tribal offices they held, served as liaison officers between the ghettos and the outside world.

The slum-dwelling Irish were not untouched by the burgeoning wealth and activity of the Industrial Revolution or by the slowly evolving social reforms of Victoria's reign. By the 1860s the Irish community had become noticeably advanced upon its previous state.

The franchise reforms of 1867, 1884, and 1885 gave the Irish a greater voice in the political future of their adopted country and enabled them to exercise an influence which could sometimes be a crucial factor at the highest level of British politics.

For some, however, the pace of constitutionalism was too slow and invited the emergence of movements which sought to achieve political change by physical force. The earliest of such revolutionary groups was the Fenian Brotherhood, otherwise known as the I.R.B., founded in 1858 and, in its militant republicanism, the precursor of the present-day I.R.A. But, like the I.R.A. today, it drew but a tiny minority of support from among the 'exiles': predictably areas of strong immigrant insularity such as districts of Lancashire and Glasgow provided the bulk of the adherents. Springing from a cultural recall of pre-Christian Gaelic Ireland, the Fenians of the mid-nineteenth-century Irish ghettos took their name from the mythological tribal guardians of a utopian time, but had to compromise at the more mundane level of arms-drilling and conspiratorial whispers of an armed uprising of the Irish in Britain.

It was never really on, of course. The mass of the immigrants, as we have seen, were too impaled upon the rigours of day-to-day survival. The former peasantry of the Irish countryside, now the urban peasants of British cities, were conditioned not to mass insurrection but rather to improve their lot by guile, labour, and petty dishonesty. The minority who were politicized were drawn off into the constitutional and radical movements of O'Connell and O'Connor. Thus when Fenian activists were arrested in Manchester in 1867, there was no 'storming of the city gates' by revolutionary hordes from the Newtown ghetto. Instead, there was the storming of a prison van, during which a constable was shot dead. His colleagues promptly saved the Irish killers from a mob bent on biblical vengeance in the streets. In November of that year three men, Allen, Larkin, and O'Brien, were hanged for the murder of the policeman and have become enshrined in the Republican conscience as the 'Manchester Martyrs'. In the month following their execution another incompetent attempt involving explosives was made to rescue a Fenian from London's Clerkenwell prison. The prisoner survived the excessive explosion from a barrel of gunpowder, but a row of nearby houses was demolished and twelve occupants died. This time there were no handy perpetrators for mob vengeance, but that evening Irishmen were pulled out of pubs in the East End and assured of their racial identity in near-by alleyways. The Clerkenwell episode provided a predictable cathartic shock. Ghetto support for the Fenians dwindled overnight, native public opinion was outraged, Irish labourers were without jobs, and the Government, among other reactions, founded an undercover branch of the constabulary to maintain surveillance over Irish and other political subversives. (Today, over a hundred years later, the lineal descendants of that police branch, now known as the DI5, keep a shadowy relationship with the lineal descendants of the Fenians, the I.R.A.)

But as well as being the precursor of twentieth-century republicanism, the short-lived tenure of the Fenians among the immigrants had significance in another direction. For the year of the abortive Fenian rising was also the year in which the vote was first given to the urban proletariat, thereby allowing the Irish in Britain to capitalize on their ghetto-grouping. Constitutionalism, as opposed to the political leverage of physical force, was given an energetic push forward. After further reforms of the franchise in 1884–5, the Irish urban masses were forming significant organized political groupings which were to have an important influence on voting patterns. By this time, too, they had become a secondary power in the Catholic Church, to the extent that Cardinal Manning in 1882 over-stated: 'I have given up working for the people of England to work for the Irish occupation of England.' The twin emancipations of the community were to dovetail upon the personality of the next radical leader of Irish opinion, Charles Stewart Parnell, who in the House of Commons headed the agitation for the Repeal of the Union, by this time known as the Home Rule movement.

Whereas O'Connell before him had drawn little from among the Irish in Britain beyond crowd support and emotional energy for the Repeal of the Union, the post-Famine influx had produced, by the 1880s, the first ethnic voting bloc. The county of Lancashire again provided the bulk of Irish support. The politician and journalist T. P. O'Connor, representing the Scotland Road constituency of Liverpool, put his vote behind Parnell. Michael Davitt, a product as much of industrial Lancashire as the famine-stricken Co. Mayo, was a vigorous propagandist within the immigrant communities. So vociferous and potent was immigrant agitation that the English hierarchy were prevailed upon to cool the political passions of their Irish congregations during the outbreaks of sectarian violence in Ireland.

The general election of 1885 saw the emergence of the ethnic vote among the Irish in Britain. Parnell's party stood for Home Rule and reform of land rents; this latter issue had great emotional sway with the immigrants, who were, for the most part, victims of such rents. The Irish vote was withdrawn from the Liberal Party; the result of the election was an eighty-six-seat victory for the Liberals over the Conservatives, but eighty-five members of Parnell's party were returned in Ireland and O'Connor was returned for the crucial seat in Liverpool. The balance of power in the subsequent parliament therefore lay with the Irish—in the final analysis with the Liverpool Irish. Faced with this unique ethnic lever, successive British governments introduced a series of measures which considerably improved the lot of Irish peasantry in Ireland, giving them in the first instance grants to purchase their smallholdings and thus free themselves from the crippling rack-rents—an important but often overlooked social and economic revolution.

By 1890, in fact, a number of extensive measures had noticeably improved the lot of Ireland in areas of academic institutions, social welfare, and rural education. In Britain, correspondingly, the means of the immigrants had considerably improved. The fortuitous power of T. P. O'Connor's ethnic vote in the Government of 1885–6 gave the impetus for a nationwide organizing of the Irish in Britain. By 1890 the Irish National League had 630 branches throughout Britain —approximately the number of seats in parliament—which lobbied for the immigrant vote on the issue of Home Rule. Although its registered members were but a minute proportion (less than a half per cent) of the immigrant population, the very fact of its existence increased their political consciousness. In parliament Parnell's party wrung concession upon concession for the welfare of Ireland and seemed on the brink of achieving the long-desired political objective of an independent self-governing island. The way seemed clear as the critical year of 1890 approached. And then the strains under the currents smashed upwards, released by a few trite phrases in a London divorce court in November 1890. Parnell was named as the co-respondent in the matrimonial action of a junior member of his own party, Captain O'Shea.

Although Parnell's liaison with Katherine O'Shea was exposed and manipulated by his political enemies, in the final analysis it was the political immaturity of his own Irish followers that cut him down. Following the divorce court proceedings, Parnell was attacked on all sides: the British Establishment, the Catholic hierarchies of England and Ireland (politically united for once), his own 'inner cabinet' (including T. P. O'Connor), ranting parish priests all over Ireland (long jealous of his sway over the people) all combined to bring down the 'Chief' and to demand his political demise. Unable to combat the hysteria of opposition, Parnell unwillingly obliged. A year later the former 'uncrowned King of Ireland'—now dethroned—was dead.

It is worthwhile to pause here and survey the progress which the Irish community had made in its settlement in Britain by

the final decade of the nineteenth century. The political cohesion of the immigrants which had been sundered by the
overthrow and death of Parnell reflected the underlying social
cohesion of the community. By this time the settlements of
the ghettos had taken root and become an accepted feature of
the larger towns and cities. The offspring of the Famine refugees, the second-generation Irish, had asserted themselves in
the community, providing social and political leadership and,
with their English accents and Irish temperament, acting as a
communicating link between more recent immigrants and the
world outside. By the 1890s the Irish had notched up over a
century of free-flowing immigration into Britain. During that
period they formed the largest ethnic minority and the most
separate single sub-group of the poor. In the reports of social
workers and welfare committees they were identified with the
poor—it could be hazarded that either the poor gave the Irish
a bad name or the Irish gave the poor a bad name. Certainly
the dovetailing of the two strata was profound and was reflected in the figures for court convictions and imprisonments,
in which both the Irish and the poor scored disproportionately
to their numbers.

As the conclusion of the nineteenth century witnessed an
improvement in the lot of the poor, so did it witness similar
improvement in the immigrants. From the days of the early
ghetto settlements they had grown with and survived the Industrial Revolution and had been touched and improved by
the powerful social forces of the era: the development of the
railways, the Ten-Hour-Day Factory Act, the compulsory education of children, and the increase in life expectancy. The
period was punctuated by the Gordon Riots at the beginning
(which left them fearful), the Stockport Riots in the middle
(which left them defiant), and the Fenian explosions of 1867
which, while begetting modern Republicanism, left the
majority unconverted to that prejudice.

By the end of the century the Irish in Britain had become a
settled community of nearly a million among a population of
thirty million. They had developed their own internal structure of community support, based mainly on the publican and
the priest. They had built their enormous Catholic churches,

published their own newspapers,[2] and were making tentative excursions out of their ghettos. In the cities they worked as labourers, costermongers, and street vendors. A lesser number continued in the privileged caste of navvies, while thousands enlisted in the British army regiments which spearheaded actions in the Crimea and in South Africa. In the political life of their adopted country they had become a force to be reckoned with and had helped induce governments to adopt a benevolent Irish policy—as a result of which there was an immense improvement in economic conditions in Ireland and a consequent reduction in emigration to Britain (although the rate of emigration to America remained high). And in the upper echelons of society, mavericks like Oscar Wilde, Bernard Shaw, and Frank Harris continued that tradition whereby Irish literati instructed the English as to how the English might best behave themselves.

As a diasporic people, the trauma of the Famine scattering was behind them. The twin prongs of fate and colonialism had pitchforked the Irish from the home-hearth across St George's Channel into the domain of the traditional enemy. Both they and the surprised native needed a breathing-space to recover from that shock encounter. The benevolent fading of the nineteenth century, with political peace in Ireland and no great social unrest in Britain, provided them both at least with that measure of racial relaxation.

[2] Although every generation since the Famine influx managed to produce a newspaper or periodical, most were short-lived. Many catered for a region, such as the *Irish Tribune* which circulated in the Newcastle area, or the *Irish Banner* in Scotland, and *Observer* in Glasgow now the *Scottish Catholic Observer*. The *Catholic Herald* also survives a century later, although no longer specifically Irish but catering to the British Catholic community at large.

Onwards from the 1900s

The period of comparative political calm between both countries which marked the opening years of the twentieth century disguised, and encouraged, the growth of what was to become the most potent influence on Anglo-Irish relations, namely Irish nationalism. Surface impressions were benevolent and deceptive. Under pressure from the Irish Parliamentary Party at Westminster, the Government's attitude to Ireland brought about increased land purchase by former tenants and a modest alleviation of the grim social conditions. The Irish version of the Industrial Revolution had brought increased employment to the towns, with a consequent drop in emigration to Britain to a level of around 20,000 annually, the lowest level since the Famine. Many of the emergent political strains in English society were mirrored in Ireland, with one salient difference. Whereas in England the new feudal structure of the industrially new rich had produced the simmering discontents of left-wing socialism, in Ireland the same rebellious philosophies now being nurtured were directed *nationalistically*. Whereas in England these forces found expression through the formation of the Labour Party, opposed to the indigenous ruling class, in Ireland the same dissident attitudes were directed against a ruling class which happened to be English in its manifestations and personnel. Whereas in England the movers of the new socialism were scornful of the social habits and mores of the 'ruling class', so in Ireland were the formulators of similar reaction scornful of similar characteristics, which were most simply seen as manifestations of *English* rule.

Accordingly, the creators of Ireland's reactionary equivalent to the British radical resentment formulated a caste of 'Gaelic Ireland' attitudes. The ancient books of legend and folklore were plundered for manifestations of an exclusive Irish culture. Any symbol imagined to be native Irish was 'in', everything symbolic of the English/Anglo-Saxon was 'out'. The movement became known as the Gaelic Revival, and like most such obsessions, was initially developed by upper- and middle-class cultural enthusiasts of Anglo-Irish ancestry like Douglas Hyde and Constance Gore-Booth. The peasantry initially reacted with scepticism to the urban obsessives who came among them, sometimes dressed in national costume to awaken them to a sense of their 'true destiny'. Nevertheless the movement flourished. The Gaelic Athletic Association, set up to foster contests 'racy of the soil', flourished in an atmosphere of discovered nationalism. No members of the British Crown Forces (military) or of the Royal Irish Constabulary (which consisted mainly of Irishmen) were allowed to participate in its contests, a rule which still applies in Northern Ireland. Douglas Hyde, who founded the Gaelic League in 1893, was to become President of the Republic which had been declared by armed rebellion in 1916. Many of those who baptized the new state in cordite were graduates of Constance Gore-Booth's Fianna Eireann boy scouts, militantly modelled on the mythological Fianna.

Thus was a revolutionary movement in Ireland formed, fashioned, and fired by recourse to malleable legend and by appeal to concepts of racial nationhood which were revived from the embers of folklore memory which had survived successive conquests. The Gaelic Revival, which incorporated the Gaelic Athletic Association, the Gaelic League, Sinn Féin (Ourselves Alone), and the Irish Republican Brotherhood, pivoted on two splendid ironies—the fact that much of the Revival was initially conceived by stalwarts of the Anglo-Irish class and the fact that its subsequent flowering was due in no little measure to the increased literacy and education brought about by a benevolent British Government.

Among a section of the immigrants to Britain, the Gaelic Revival took firm root. The first few years of the 1900s, while showing a drastic reduction in immigrant numbers, were also witness to the influx of what, for want of a better term, one may call middle-class immigrants. They came particularly to join the Civil Service, having sat the entrance examinations in Ireland. Two such candidates, who were later to become prominent in affairs in Ireland, were Michael Collins and Sam Maguire. The writers Padraic O'Conaire and Peadar Kearney worked in London at the same time, and the poet William Butler Yeats lived in Kensington and presided over the Irish Literary Society—in London! In near-by West Kensington, Michael Collins was employed in the Post Office as a clerk and, with fellow Corkonian Sam Maguire, founded a unit of the I.R.B., using for arms drill Post Office rifles stored in the event of a German invasion. Constance Gore-Booth, as befitting her lineage, was presented at Court as a debutante and was escorted in London Society by young army subalterns upon whom later she was to pull, literally, a blazing revolver in Dublin.

In Britain the ripples of the Gaelic Revival touched settled families of Irish descent, notably in Liverpool, Edinburgh, and Glasgow. Two of such lineal immigrant descent were James Connolly and Jim Larkin, both of whom spent formative years among the ghetto communities, went 'home' to Ireland and were subsequently to become powerful influences upon political and labour movements. James Connolly founded the Irish Citizen Army, probably the first 'people's militia' in these islands, consisting mainly of trade unionists and workers with a specific anti-captitalist bias which was nonetheless drawn into active service in the Rising of 1916. His colleague from among the Irish in Britain, Jim Larkin, founded a trade union and both came to be regarded as the creative conscience of developing left-wing Labour philosophy in Ireland. Subsequently influential in their own particular way were Constance Gore-Booth, Douglas Hyde, the poet Yeats, and the future guerrilla-leader Michael Collins. All were part of the London Irish at the turn of the century.

Rarely has an émigré community welded together such disparate elements and formed in exile the future military, political, and cultural leaders of a new state. The unifying link was the ethos of the Gaelic Revival, which began as the cultural dalliance of the socially privileged, sounded echoes among the depressed lower-middle classes in Ireland and immigrant families in Britain; reverberated in the tolling of racial recall among the peasantry; and finally unleashed the potent force of Irish nationalism which gave birth to the Irish Republic in 1916.

If the lives of these luminaries among the immigrants in the early 1900s were irretrievably bound up with the Gaelic Revival, the lives of the majority of the immigrants were, as usual, not so diverted. For the majority, the day-to-day demands of ordinary experience were more important than the abstractions of nationalistic endeavour. It is true they were affected by the revival of nationalism, but in a cursory manner as a conversational topic for the majority, or perhaps attendance at an Irish Language class for a tiny minority. For most, the improvement of their social and economic lot was the prime consideration. Whereas the peak years of nineteenth-century emigration to Britain had been occasioned by the Great Famine and its aftermath, now at the beginning of the twentieth century, the settled pattern of immigration had economic and social roots; the desire for higher wages and better opportunities for individual improvement was the criterion of arrival in Britain. Wages, social conditions, educational opportunities for their children were what mattered more than the idealistic concepts of the Gaelic Ireland of the nationalists. The anti-Irish hostility of the immediate post-Famine decades had substantially diminished by the early 1900s; as mentioned earlier, the 'Irish' had become an accepted part of working-class communities, and they in turn welcomed and thrived on the changed degree of acceptance. The advent of the First World War, with Britain rallying regiments to the defence of the 'small nations', provided a conflicting pull and was to set a choice of loyalties before the Irish in Britain. Overwhelmingly, they cast their loyalty for Britain, and over 150,000 Irishmen fought in the war. Among the Irish in Britain, battalions were raised in Glasgow, Edinburgh, London, and Tyneside. From London the regiments of the Irish Guards and the London-Irish Rifles drew heavily on first and second generation Irish, thereby consolidating the tradition of émigré service in the British Army. The majority of the immigrants decided the 'freedom of the small nations' to be of more immediate import than the distant possible freedom of a more intimate 'small nation'. The apparently insoluble differences among Irishmen regarding politics in their own country were shelved for the duration of the European conflict. Their attitude was cogently expressed in an account of the charge of the London Irish at Loos, published in the *Weekly Dispatch* of October 1915. It began:

HOW THE LONDON IRISH SAVED AN ARMY CORPS
New Regiment's Glorious Rush and Stand at Battle of Loos
Football dribbled into enemy trench

'We were all kinds and creeds and parties in the regiment, and we often thought how only a little over a year ago we were on the point of civil war. But this war has taught us the oneness of the Empire; so you saw landlord and peasant, Catholic and Protestant, Unionist and Nationalist, all friendly as probably never before in Irish history, and all vowing vengeance on the Hun.'

However, some who fought abroad for the Empire returned to Ireland, to take up arms against their former British Army colleagues and to participate in the Rising of 1916, declared on the ancient thesis that 'England's difficulty was Ireland's opportunity'. The Rising and the subsequent Anglo-Irish War of 1919–21 proved heavily divisive among the Irish in Britain, most of whom now had some degree of loyalty to Britain and were bewildered by the Rising. Predictably, this division of loyalties was most severe in the traditional immigrant areas of the larger cities. In Glasgow, the immigrants' paper, *The Observer*, declared that the Rising was the 'madly criminal action of pro-German plotters'. Unswayed by such condemnation, units of the I.R.A. in Glasgow drilled and trained under the command of former British Army servicemen, using as a handbook the Army training manual; men and women from the city went to Ireland to involve themselves in the Rising and its aftermath of guerrilla war, and guns and ammunition were transferred to Dublin in appropriate containers of coffins ostensibly holding returned remains of immigrants. By 1920, the I.R.A. register in Glasgow numbered 4,000 recruits and the financial contribution from among the Scottish communities was reckoned by de Valera to be in excess of funds from any other country, including Ireland.

The London Irish who had provided detachments of I.R.A. volunteers to aid the Rising turned out in their thousands when the I.R.A. detachment escorted the emaciated body of Terence McSwiney from Brixton Prison to Southwark Cathedral (built by the contribution of the immigrant poor) where it lay in state. McSwiney, Republican Lord Mayor of Cork, died after seventy-four days on hunger strike in protest against the activities of the Black and Tans in Ireland. His funeral procession was an emotive affair, but it is doubtful if more than a minority of the hundred thousand Irish who lined the London streets agreed with the sacrificial nature of his republicanism or sympathized with his concept of the need for armed struggle. Not the least of their many conflicting reactions may have been the thought that, for most of them, the simple act of emigrant transference across the Irish Sea had brought the material and social benefits which McSwiney and his colleagues hoped their militant sacrifice would eventually bestow upon Ireland. Sadly, the post-revolutionary Irish Government did not fulfil the ideals of vastly improved living standards and opportunities. In the 1920s, of course, such disillusion harboured in the distant future, and the immigrants were sufficiently sceptical of miracles being wrought. Accordingly they paid easy lip service to the idea of an Ireland free of British rule, while determining that their own interests might best be served by remaining in Britain. Even the subsequent ratification of an Irish Free State incurred no great rushing 'home' from among the 750,000 Irish-born in Britain.

Rather were the immigrants determinedly consolidating their claim upon Britain, becoming involved at many levels of indigenous life. Socially, they formed a weighty rump of the working classes, politically they supported the growing Labour Party and in the inherited tradition of Feargus O'Connor's radicalism, the newly-formed Communist Party of Great Britain in 1920 numbered three of Irish descent[1] among its founders. In the traditionally radically-oriented communities of Lancashire they were prominent in the growth of trade

[1] J. T. Murphy, Tom Bell, Arthur McManus.

unions and nationwide they formed the backbone of Roman Catholic religious expansion. They had, indeed, little to complain of in their absorption into the passive mainstream of British life.

There were, of course, repercussions from the native population arising from the vicissitudes of the war in Ireland and the reactions to charge and counter-charge of brutality which emanated in newspaper reports from Ireland. When, in November 1920, the execution 'squad' of the former Kensington Post Office clerk, Michael Collins (now commander of the anti-British guerrilla forces), shot fourteen British army officers in Dublin, the interiors of several 'Irish' public houses in working-class districts of London were smashed up by infuriated Cockney mobs. There were also some attempts to damage Catholic churches. Members of the I.R.A. in Britain later 'retaliated' by firing warehouses on Tyneside and smashing shop windows in London's Oxford Street, but the mass of the immigrants remained but little affected by the bloody bitterness of the war; many of them, anyway, had seen sufficient of war's destruction in the service of the Empire.

Collins himself—having headed an I.R.A. guerrilla campaign in Ireland which brought the political leaders of the two nations to the conference table—arrived in London as part of the Irish negotiating team which faced, among others, the British premier Lloyd George and Winston Churchill. Tumultuous crowds of the London Irish turned out to 'welcome back' the Commander-in-Chief of the I.R.A., and among those with whom he renewed acquaintance was his sister, Joanna Collins, who had calmly stayed at her London desk in the Civil Service while her brother had returned to wage war on the British administration in Ireland.

The conference was marked by a formal cessation of hostilities in Ireland to encourage as calm as possible an atmosphere. Although the calm was very nearly shattered by an attempt by some members of the Irish Guards—a regiment which had lost almost 2,500 men and acquired four Victoria Crosses in the war—to steal guns from the regimental depot for the I.R.A. a treaty was finally negotiated and ratified by both Parliaments. It consigned twenty-six counties to freedom from British sovereignty. The remaining six counties were to become—and currently are—the subject of bitter dispute, the subsequent course of which, however, was to have little effect on the Irish in Britain. By 1928, Irish immigrants were entering Britain at a steady pace which reflected the incompetence of the post-revolutionary Irish governments and provided, by their emigration, ample evidence for those who held the views that 'the Irish were incapable of governing themselves'. Even with the effects of the Land Act of the previous year, which divided up the former estates of absentee landlords, the immigration of the Irish to Britain continued at a substantial rate. Those who came were for the most part from rural areas and followed the traditional occupations; the men in labouring and navvying, the women in domestic service.

Effects of the British-sponsored educational improvements were, however, to be perceived in the growth of what was colloquially referred to as 'a better class of immigrant', in the influx of graduates of the National University of Ireland, the successor of the Catholic University founded in Dublin by the English Cardinal Newman. This increased influx of graduates, mainly doctors and dentists, did not, however, receive a welcome from the equivalent stratum of the host society. Anti-Irish resentment occasioned by the Rising of 1916—seen by many middle-class British as a 'stab in the back' during the war with Germany—lingered well into the 1920s and was to some extent intensified by the Anglo-Irish Treaty of 1921. Thus many of the Irish Catholic graduates who came to Britain in the immediate post-Treaty years were regarded as disloyal Sinn Féiners who now had the temerity to seek professional positions in a country whose sovereignty over Ireland had been rejected. Many Irish graduates found themselves unwelcome in the London clubs which catered for the professions—and they reacted by forming a separate club for Irish graduates in Britain. This was the National University of Ireland Club, initially with premises near Westminster Cathedral, later to become a favourite location of Irish middle-class clubs and societies. Following the severe class prejudices of the time, the graduates formed a self-congratulatory ghetto, separated from the Irish working-class ghettos, not by either accent or temperament, but rather by would-be social status. The graduates were understandably sensitive as to their precise social status in a society which functioned rigidly on such distinctions.

Such were the pressures of the late 1920s for the 'better-educated class of immigrant' who came in increasing proportions, sensitive to the stock judgements of a society which saw all 'Irish' immigrants in the cast of Punch cartoon characters.

We can imagine the effects upon a member of the University Club, had he purchased in London's Charing Cross Road 'a book for children' of the 1920s, which contained this verse:

> The Irish Child can dance a jig
> And share its pillow with a pig
> And where we ask for pie or meat
> The praties he is glad to eat.

It is understandable that they and other Irish professional men would seek to separate themselves from the mass of working-class immigrants. Although the graduate body could be held to be the natural leaders of the immigrant community, the social divisions which they condoned militated against any efforts to alleviate the depressed state of the mass of immigrants. Had they been able to overcome the separatist social pressures of the host societies, it is fair to say that inroads could have been made upon these 'social problems' of drunkenness, unemployment, lack of vocational direction which characterized their working-class compatriots, making them figure disproportionately in criminal and health statistics: in the 1930s the contribution from among the immigrant Irish to the total prison population did not fall below 20 per cent when they hardly numbered 2 per cent of the population. Native newspapers were not reticent in identifying the nationality of those who appeared before the courts or who formed a substantial proportion of those treated for tuberculosis in British hospitals. The Famine imagery still sounded echoes and some of the tensions of that era were revived with the Depression of the early 1930s.

This lack of community leadership was the greatest single

deficiency which the immigrants suffered. The homeland of the time, by contrast, began to formulate progressive economic and social measures, albeit in the face of meagre human and financial resources and with the burden of an inexperienced administration. At a time when, as Seán O'Faoláin has recorded, 'the Catholic Church was felt, feared and courted on all sides as the dominant power', with attendant inhibiting effects upon progressive social policies. For the Irish workers in Britain there was a profound absence of social leadership, rendering them as mere factory and building-site fodder, totally at the whim of economic forces. Only in the traditional immigrant areas of Scotland and the North-East was there in existence the semblance of a receiving community structure into which they could absorb with confidence, being the continuum of previous generations' activity in community and trade union affairs.

1930s

Accordingly, it was in these areas, notably Liverpool, Newcastle, Rochdale, and Leeds, that many rural Irish began to consolidate their claim upon the host country, against a background of Depression fears of the thirties. In this they were aided by the staunch friendships of the descendants of previous generations of immigrants who were strong in the local Catholic and working-class communities. In other areas, by comparison, there was little encouragement to settle; it was not uncommon, for instance, for factories in the Coventry and Birmingham regions to display 'No Irish need apply' signs alongside notices of vacancies. Similar declarations were prominent on accommodation notice-boards in parts of Scotland with the added rider of 'No Catholics'. One can only hazard at the mixed feelings of the Irish Protestant immigrants—who formed a steady trickle of the overall immigration—to such notices.

It is hardly surprising, then, that the Irish conformed to the previous century's pattern of seeking shelter in the most run-down and dilapidated districts; the men sleeping two to a bed in overcrowded rooms, for which privilege they paid £1 a week in 1938, when the average industrial weekly wage was £5.

There was more private, if rudimentary, accommodation in Camden Town's Rowton House, a hostel barracks of the Railway Age. Patrick Kavanagh, the poet of bitter, barren, rural Ireland, stayed there for a time during his 'literary emigration' to London in 1935, and afterwards wrote that: 'many Irish boys made Rowton House, Camden Town, first stop from Mayo. The soft voices of Mayo and Galway sounding in that gaunt, impersonal place fell like warm rain on the arid patches of my imagination.' His compatriots in Rowton House, Kavanagh judged to be 'true peasants. They walked with an awkward gait and were shy. To me they looked up as to a learned man and posed me crooked questions which I couldn't answer ... I had seen too much of them in Ireland. Their characters, impressionable as wax, were soon to wear the impress of common vulgarity.' The poet did not take to London; his heart lay in the rejected rural reaches, and with pastoral imagery he perhaps articulated the feelings of his 'true peasants' when he wrote:

> London is a pagan city, and it is not the poetic paganism of blackbirds. After the chaste paganism of Ireland London's materialistic immorality terrified me.... There was little innocent courting: on Hampstead Heath I saw them copulating like dogs in the sun.... I returned to Ireland. Ireland green and chaste and foolish. And when I wandered over my own hills and talked again to my own people, I looked into the heart of this life and I saw that it was good.[2]

For most of the inhabitants of Rowton House there was no such happy return to Ireland 'green and chaste' but rather the immigrant grind ahead. Their social gathering places were, predictably, the public houses, and they felt at ease only in the most scruffy of these premises. As an immigrant 'community' of labourers, porters, and navvies, they felt as put-upon and as subject to native resentment as their antecedents of the Famine

[2]Patrick Kavanagh, *The Green Fool*, London: Martin Brian & O'Keeffe, 1971.

diaspora. They suffered profoundly, as has been mentioned, from lack of concern from some of their better-off country-men. One veteran of the thirties, now a prosperous building contractor in London, recalled for me the severity of divisions between the working-class Irish and 'professional' Irish:

There was simply no meaningful contact. We stuck to our circuit and they stuck to theirs. Occasionally, we might meet an Irish architect or doctor at some Church function, but they always struck me as being embarrassed when we met and when I told them I was a carpenter ... though we both had our best suits on and no doubt could have had a lot in common to talk about ... but I sensed their tightness, somehow. Mind you, I was from Mayo, and these people would be from a city such as Dublin or Cork. Perhaps, look-ing back on it, I was extra-sensitive myself, country people always are, you know. We think the 'city slicker' is looking down on us. I remember at dances now, I'd take a girl up that might be from my part of the country and I'd say 'where are you from?' and she'd put on this awfully, you know, accent and say, 'I'm from Dublin, actually'. And she'd probably be a maid or waitress ... or something like that.

Mind you, we were all very sensitive and unsure then. We'd cling together a lot with lads from our own county. After Mass we'd go to a pub in Leeds frequented by Mayo men. The talk would be mostly about Mayo and who was doing what back there—or about Mayo men here, and what they were doing in the 'diggin's'. After that we might have a meal, but never in a place that looked 'proper', with table-cloths and so on. We'd be scared to go into a place like that, even on Sunday with our best suits on, in case they'd throw us out for not knowing how to behave properly at table. We all shared rooms in digs, and sometimes we shared beds—but no immorality mind you—and sent money home most weeks and said we were getting on fine at the buildin'—even though in the thirties we'd have work only about three weeks out of four. When you met someone you knew, the remark always was 'Are ye workin'?' It was up to yourself to get work when it was scarce, by letting on to a foreman what a great worker you could be if you were given a job. Some fellows used to develop a particular way of walking, coming onto a site to look for work—they called it 'The Gimp'—it amounted to a sort of swagger which gave an impression of confidence. When a fellow with 'The Gimp' came onto a site, he'd kick any ould timber outa his way— fuck it outa his way, as much as to say: 'You want a tunnel dug ... I'll dig it myself in a day ...'

And then coming to England with the lads and sticking together, being afraid to talk to the English girls, and all the time this brooding thing of history ... well, it didn't help in so-called integrating, I was fifteen years here before I came to know English people properly—and that only happened when I started up my own business, and met them as an equal, in a manner of speaking. Now, I'll tell you something. I'd prefer to do business with an Englishman any day of the week; they're more honest than the Irish and they keep their discretion as well as their delivery dates. And they don't have the malice the Irish have towards each other, resenting the fellow that gets on in the world ... resenting the fellow who pulls himself up out of the spite.

Sometimes now I go for a stroll around Camden Town, after Mass on a Sunday, and the lads are still there, just like I was in Leeds all them years ago, only now they're in Greek and Eyetalian cafes, having their Sunday grub, because they're not wanted in the digs. I look at them, all atin' away without a word between them, stuffin' mixed grills down their gollops ... and I'm glad them days are behind me.

You ask me if there was any Community help? Ah, you're jokin' using phrases like that. What Community? We relied on ourselves. We felt we were only tolerated by the English, by landladies and such ... and by employers because we were good at digging. Sometimes, if we were feeling belligerent, which usually followed on feeling miserable, we'd go to an 'English' pub, waiting to hear some crack about 'the Paddies' or 'the Micks'—looking for an excuse to start a barney, you know.

Looking back on it now, thirty years afterwards, I can see

what was wrong with us. Now that I've had a bit of time to read and think about these things, I can see we were too wrapped up in ourselves. In a way we suffered from two things: coming from rural Ireland and from the education we had there. In the country, you see, we hardly ever met English people, and our Christian Brother[3] education was very anti-British ... The Black and Tans and 1920 and all that sort of thing.

It was a case of every man for himself during the week, and then the pub on Sunday where you could pretend to be friends again.

I'll tell you one thing though. It made us look out for ourselves, made us self-reliant.

Apart from the efforts of some individual priests, the only concerted effort to combat the 'hard times' of the thirties appears to have come from the Connolly Association in London, which in 1935 produced the paper, *Irish Freedom* (later re-named the *Irish Democrat*) which urged its readers to join trade unions and to absorb the heady philosophy of the socialist James Connolly, executed for his part in the 1916 Rising. It was also on the lookout for instances of discrimination against Irish workers, without having many resources to combat them beyond publicizing the circumstances of such cases.

The founders of the Connolly Association toured Britain in pursuit of their efforts to politicize immigrant workers towards left-wing socialism, tirelessly banging their political heads on two brick walls of ingrained cultural resistance: the innate caution of most Irish workers and the antagonism of Irish priests, who often warned from the pulpit against the Connolly Association. (One of the Association's founders, Desmond Greaves, in fact personally encouraged his followers to attend their religious services.)

By 1938, with the advent of war with Germany but a year away, more militant demands were being made upon some of the immigrants to join the I.R.A., with the promise of 'action' in Britain when hostilities with Germany began. But that

[3] A religious order of stern disciplinarians which has dominated the education of most Southern Irish males during the past century.

organization made even less headway than the Connolly Association among the immigrants. Most of the I.R.A. 'bombers' who waged the subsequent cruel Bombing Campaign upon the civilian population in Britain came over specifically from Ireland to do so; the mass of the immigrants did not see much point in abusing the hospitality of their hosts. In spite of their disavowal of such activities, the Bombing Campaign nevertheless affected their shaky relationship with the host community, as did the Republic's policy of neutrality during the war. It is worth briefly tracing these twin developments in relation to the Irish in Britain.

The I.R.A. bombing campaign sprang directly from the Anglo-Irish Treaty of 1921, which conceded, as we have seen, self-determination to twenty-six of Ireland's thirty-two counties. The remaining six, because of the inherited militant loyalty to Britain of the majority of the inhabitants (descendants of Protestant-Scots planters since the sixteenth century), remained within the United Kingdom. The Treaty, though ratified by the Irish Parliament (the Dáil), resulted in civil war in the Free State. Through the 1920s and 1930s those who held fast to that ideal of a thirty-two-county Republic engaged in sporadic military enterprise. Britain's war with Germany reactivated the I.R.A. to old campaigning. Three years before the outbreak of the Second World War, an I.R.A. leader on a visit to America declared the intention of waging a 'military' campaign on Britain, in the event of hostility between Britain and Germany. He was, in part, succumbing to Irish-American euphoria, a legacy bequeathed by Famine folklore to the New World. Said the I.R.A. leader, Sean Russell: (1) When hostilities start we shall certainly send 'planes to bomb England. (2) We also have quantities of ammunition and other war materials in England. (3) In England ... we have another secret army of Irishmen who meet quietly for drill and target practice.

Comment on the actual reality behind these claims is salutary, for it illustrates the mixture of naïvety and self-deception which led to the Bombing Campaign: (1) The I.R.A. had no 'planes. (2) The total armaments of the I.R.A. in Britain amounted to less than two dozen assorted firearms. (3) The 'secret army of Irishmen' amounted to less than a hundred ill-trained juveniles and adults out of a total Irish population of 850,000.

Nevertheless, the campaign got off to a fatal start and a Mancunian worker died when a sewer was blasted with a time-bomb. This was rapidly followed by a series of further explosions aimed against innocent civilians as home-made but lethal bombs went off in litter-bins, subway stations, and left-luggage booths at main-line stations, maiming and crippling bystanders and passers-by. After fifty-four such attacks in London, the Government brought in the Prevention of Violence Bill in July 1939 which compelled Irishmen in Britain to register with the police—a lineal descendant of a government order of four hundred years previously to contain the problem of Irish vagrants. The Special Branch and Scotland Yard made weekly arrests, aided by the amateurism of their prey, many of whom were adolescents. Some of them stored large quantities of potassium chlorate in their 'digs', and were duly given away by landladies. Others, purchasing 'alarum' clocks—which triggered the explosives of which potassium was part—were politely asked to wait by shop assistants who then telephoned the police. These young I.R.A. men, brought up in that narrow Republican religion which laid the cause of all Ireland's ills at Britain's door, took to the more militant forms of republicanism at an age when many adolescents develop a zealous philosophy of some kind.

One of these adolescents was the sixteen-year-old Brendan Behan, playwright-to-be, whose subsequent best-selling novel *Borstal Boy*, opens with an account of his arrest in Liverpool:

Friday, in the evening, the landlady shouted up the stairs: 'Oh God, oh Jesus, oh Sacred Heart. Boy, there's two gentlemen to see you.'

I knew by the screeches of her that these gentlemen were not calling to inquire after my health, or to know if I'd had a good trip. I grabbed my suitcase, containing Pot. Chlor, Sulph Ac, gelignite, detonators, electrical and ignition, and the rest of my Sinn Fein conjuror's outfit, and carried it to the window. Then the gentlemen arrived.

A young one, with a blond, Herrenvolk head and a B.B.C.

accent shouted, 'I say, greb him, the bestud.'

When I was safely grabbed, the blond one gave me several punches in the face, though not very damaging ones. An older man, in heavy Lancashire speech, told him to leave me alone, and to stop making a —— of himself.... There were now two or three others in the room, and this old man was the sergeant and in charge of the raid.

He took some Pot. Chlor and sugar out of the case, put it in the empty fireplace and lit it with a match. It roared into flame and filled the room with smoke. He nodded to me and I nodded back.

Saxonhead and another, a quiet fellow, had me gripped by the arms.

'Got a gun, Paddy?' asked the sergeant.

'If I'd have had a gun you wouldn't have come through that door so shagging easy.'

He looked at me and sighed, as if I had said nothing, or as if he had not heard me.

'Turn him over,' he told the quiet one.

Blondie began to search me with violence.

'No, not you,' said the Sergeant, 'Vereker'. Vereker searched me, quietly, and, even along the seams of my flies, with courtesy.

'Lift your arms up over your head. Put your leg up. Thank you.'

From an inside pocket he took my money, a forged travel permit, and a letter which happened to be written in Irish.

It was from a boy in Dublin who was sick in bed and wanted me to come and see him. He was a dreary bastard in any language, and I, a good-natured and affectionate boy, found him distressing to meet and embarrassing to avoid. I would have a good excuse for not meeting him for some time to come.

The blond studied the Gaelic writing over Vereker's shoulder.

Disgusted, he turned to me and shouted, 'You facquing bestud, how would you like to see a woman cut in two by a plate-glass window?'

I would have answered him on the same level—Bloody

Sunday, when the Black and Tans attacked a football crowd in our street; the massacre at Cork; Balbriggan; Amritsar; the R.A.F. raids on Indian villages. I had them all off, and was expecting something like this. But the sergeant said in a reasonable tone:

'Well, Paddy, there are people gathered round this house, and I don't think they mean you any good.' He laughed a bit. 'But take no heed of them. We'll get you to the Assizes all right. Safe and sound.'

Vereker released my arm and went to the window.

'Uniformed men are making them move along.'

The sergeant told Blondie to let me go.

'We'll sit here a while', he said, sitting on the side of the bed, grunting. He pointed, and I came over and sat beside him.

'I wish to Christ I was your age, Paddy, I'd had something better to do than throwing bombs around. How old are you?'

'I'm sixteen, and I'll be seventeen in February.'

Behan's bombs did not go off: but he did—to Borstal. Liverpool was one city to witness immediate results of the campaign, with outbreaks of communal violence; Glasgow and Edinburgh saw similar inter-communal incidents as a result. The worst explosion occurred in Coventry in August 1939, a month before the outbreak of war when a bomb left in the carrier of a cycle in the main shopping thoroughfare of Broadgate exploded with the loss of five lives and the maiming of another twelve. Among the dead was an eighty-two-year-old man, and in the nature of such tragedies, a girl of twenty-one, due to be married a fortnight hence. Two days later, I.R.A. prisoners in Dartmoor had to be hospitalized as the result of beatings by other inmates. Subsequently two Irishmen, Barnes and McCormick, were executed for the offence, but the man who actually planted the bomb escaped. As recently as 1970, listeners to the B.B.C. midday news programme heard that man in a recorded broadcast from Dublin, say feelingly:

Ah, poor Barnes, poor Barnes, he was innocent, you know.

Such indulgence in pathos—from the safety of Ireland—must have sounded unfeelingly brutal to English listeners. Certainly the campaign provoked outbreaks of hostility against the Irish in Britain, a hostility which survives today in sparse pockets. (In 1969 a feud in the Fulham area of London, between an Irish publican and some local villains, erupted into shooting and maiming: the ill-feeling was compounded in part by the thirty-year-old memory of an I.R.A. explosive cache found in Fulham during the campaign. Fulham, an area of tightly-knit Cockney families, had been the object of repeated German bombing during the war.)

In the face of alienation of the British population, the bombing campaign lasted a year, involving around 200 explosions, the death and injury of civilians, the jailing of eighty Irishmen —some of whom never quite recovered from the incarceration —and the removal of tons of explosives from lodging houses in Irish districts of Manchester, London, Liverpool, Glasgow, and Birmingham. The effects upon the Irish in Britain were to linger well into the fifties. The immediate effect at the time was to question the 'loyalty' of the three-quarters of a million Irish who worked in Britain throughout the war effort, notably at civilian level in the munitions factories and in the construction of aerodromes, and at military level in the forces. The trustworthiness of the immigrant Irish was questioned by Winston Churchill at meetings of the war cabinet (at which Churchill probably had the advice of his Minister of Information, the Tipperary-born Brendan Bracken, on the subject). The trustworthiness of the 150,000 Irishmen in the forces was not (as far as we know) raised by the Prime Minister who was later to praise 'the temper and instincts of the thousands of Irishmen who hastened to the battle-front to prove their ancient valour'.

A longer-term effect of the Bombing Campaign upon the Irish community generally was that democratic tarring of all birds with the same brush, most starkly seen in the reluctance to promote Irish-born to supervisory or management positions in various areas of business for years afterwards, so that many were held back from personal development and usefulness. An additional element was provided by the running verbal and diplomatic battle between Churchill and Irish Prime Minister de Valera throughout the war over the use of Southern Irish 'treaty ports'.

This issue lay, as do so many contemporary issues, in the Anglo-Irish Treaty of 1921; one of the provisions of that Treaty being that Britain continued to have strategic naval bases in the Irish Republic, notably on the south-western Irish coast which looked out on to the Atlantic shipping routes. By 1938, however, de Valera, possibly with an eye to impending hostilities, had negotiated the 'return' of the ports.

Churchill was furious at the *fait accompli* and took the view that the Irish Government had repudiated the Treaty of 1921 over the issue of the ports, in that the handing back had not been ratified by the Westminster parliament. With the Republic's declaration of neutrality, and the necessity of keeping the shipping-lanes free from German harassment, the issue of the ports became critical.

The British population at large was bewildered by Ireland's policy of neutrality and angered by her refusal to grant British access to the ports—anger heightened when the German U-boats began to take their deadly toll of shipping ferrying vital war supplies to Britain via the Atlantic artery. The North Atlantic, by contrast, was protected by the Sunderland aircraft which patrolled those routes from bases in Ulster. Writing to his Dominions Secretary, who dealt with Éire, Churchill in January 1941 said:

> No attempt should be made to conceal from Mr de Valera the depth and intensity of feeling against the policy of Irish neutrality ... should the present situation last until the end of the war ... a gulf will have opened between Northern and Southern Ireland which it will be impossible to bridge in this generation.

Even with the drastic fatalities which British ships incurred off the Irish coast, the Dublin Government stuck hard by its policy. On 21 March 1941, reacting to heavy losses of ships in the Atlantic, Churchill suggested to his First Lord of the Admiralty that radar installations (by then being rapidly developed) could be set up on Tory Island, off the Donegal coast, and possibly on some islands off the Kerry coast. His scheme to gain access to the islands was that they 'might be leased privately by some wealthy American friends'.

The British advanced developments of radar techniques may have had a side-effect upon Ireland's neutrality. After the year June 1940–June 1941, when Britain suffered over 43,381 dead and 50,856 wounded through bomb attacks, British scientists developed a radar system of deflecting the radio beams which German pilots used to guide them to British cities. An effect of the deflectionary technique was to direct enemy bombs away from inhabited areas and on to open country; which may have accounted for German bombs falling upon parts of Dublin and Co. Wexford. This brought due apologies from the Axis Powers, but nevertheless tested the conviction of the Irish Government to remain neutral.

The Irish Government, though scrupulously maintaining the balance of official neutrality, was, when the balance occasionally tilted, 'neutral in favour of Britain', not least in keeping open the food routes to Britain and in the tacit encouragement throughout the war of the steady departure of emigrants to Britain facilitated by a U.K. permit office opened in Dublin. The office also directed the workers to specific areas as a condition of admission to Britain.

The permit office was administered with the co-operation of the Dublin Government and in the early years of war, emigrant batches of upwards of two thousand a week were strategically directed to parts of Britain—hardly the act of a totally neutral government. As a result of the earlier I.R.A. activity, all the Irish immigrants were required to register with the police and report any changes of address or occupation. It being wartime, all the labour force was strategically deployed; the Irish being assigned to harvest gathering, aerodrome construction, bombed-building demolition, and munitions factories in the Midlands, the last location providing an ironic postscript to Churchill's displeasure at being denied the use of southern Irish ports. During the same month as he wrote stiff letters to his staff regarding the ports, the arms-factories in Small Heath, Birmingham—earlier the object of Churchill's pressing interest—increased their rifle production through the substantial addition of Irish immigrant labour. Neither was the Irish membership of the armed forces insignificant, a contribution duly acknowledged at the end of the war by Churchill, in his victory broadcast of 13 May 1945, when he contrasted the attitude of the Irish Government with that of Irishmen who had fought in the war. Churchill said:

> We had only the North-Western approach between Ulster and Scotland through which to bring the means of life and to send out the forces of war. Owing to the action of the Dublin Government, so much at variance with the temper and instincts of thousands of Southern Irishmen who hastened to the battle front ... the approaches which the Southern Irish ports and airfields could so easily have guarded, were closed by the hostile aircraft and U-boats. This was indeed a deadly moment in our life, and if it had not been for the loyalty and friendship of Northern Ireland we should have been forced to come to close quarters or perish far from the earth. However, with a restraint and poise to which, I say, history will find few parallels, His Majesty's Government never laid a violent hand on them ... When I think of these days I also think of other episodes and personalities. I think of Lieutenant-Commander Esmonde, V.C., or Lance Corporal Keneally, V.C., and Captain Fegen, V.C., and other Irish heroes whose names I could easily recite, and then I must confess that bitterness by Britain against the Irish race dies in my heart.

Irrespective of this death of 'bitterness against the Irish race', one immediate post-war effect upon the Irish in Britain was to give them a sense of involvement in the general spectrum of British life. The comradeship which many developed in the fight for King and Country was reflected in business and personal relationships after the war. Many an Irish soldier found subsequent employment through the good offices of a wartime officer; some went into business partnership with former comrades-in-arms, notably in the construction field, which now enjoyed a post-war boom of rebuilding. Another effect was the comparative 'reduction' of class-barriers and the assumption to power of the Labour Party, with whom the Irish felt some degree of affinity; the city of Birmingham which contained a substantial Irish community returned a 23 per cent swing to Labour in the 1945 general election.

There were many other changes which encouraged the Irish to feel part of post-war Britain. The effects of the Education Act of 1944, which ensured equality of treatment to all religious denominations, could be observed in the increased building of Catholic schools, and the Irish benefited equally from the successive acts of parliament which brought about the Welfare State.[4] During the war, wages had gone up considerably; an immediate post-war effect was the heightened resumption of immigration from Ireland to employment in the building sites and factories. Even the footloose were better off on the dole in England than in Ireland: Britain offered double the unemployment money. The vast majority, of course, came to work and to claim a stake in the new Britain, and many were pleasantly surprised to find that the post-war sense of common weal encouraged that attitude.

Out of this involvement came the founding of the Irish Club in London's Eaton Square, an area more commonly identified with the aristocracy, by a group of Irishmen who met sometime in 1947 in a hostelry by the Bank of England and decided that a focal monument of similar impact was required as a gesture to the future presence of the Irish. The substantial premises in Eaton Square, almost equidistant from Buckingham Palace and Westminster Cathedral, were acquired with the aid of a donation from the Guinness family in 1948—the year that the state of Éire formally declared herself a Republic. The initial membership of the Eaton Square club reflected the post-war growth of a weighty middle-class element among the immigrants with some attendant social pretensions.

One personality who refused to join was Bernard Shaw, ever impatient with the sentimentality of the exiles. In a characteristic reply by postcard, Shaw declared:

[4] By the end of 1946 the National Health Act, the National Insurance Act, and the National Assistance Act had been initiated, thereby radically upgrading the lot of the working classes generally and providing another powerful 'pull' factor upon Irish immigration to Britain.

I can imagine nothing less desirable than an Irish Club. Irish people in England should join English clubs, and avoid each other like the plague.

If they flock together like geese they might as well have never left Ireland.

They don't admire, nor even like one another. In English clubs they are always welcome. More fools the English perhaps; but the two are so foreign that they have much to learn from their association and co-operation.

The Irish Club in fact became less introspective than Shaw might have imagined; reflecting the composite interests of retired brigadiers, nouveau riche owners of building firms, and businessmen intent on bridging historical suspicions. It was a concerted effort on behalf of middle-class immigrants to upgrade the popular residual image of Irish immigrants, or in the words of one long-time member, the Club was an effort to 'show the English that we weren't all navvies and chambermaids'—a double-edged comment hardly likely to endear the Club to the mass of working-class Irish. The Club did help 'bridge the gap' in the ensuing years between the immigrant classes, and later effected a wider diplomatic function; although an Irish Embassy became established in near-by Belgravia (in a former town-house of the Guinness family) a year after the Club became operational, the Club in fact functioned as a mini-embassy in many respects and was to be a hidden, but not insignificant, influence in subsequent Anglo-Irish relations. Not the least of its contributions was in creating the tradition whereby British and Irish Ministers of State became guests of honour at the annual St Patrick's Day dinner, thereby providing useful facilities for relaxed meetings between both governments. Nevertheless its existence, and pretensions, aroused strong feelings in the Irish community. A former Club Chairman, Noel O'Connell, provides this view of Shaw's postcard refusal to join:

The Founding Fathers of the Irish Club were incurable optimists. They created the Club in a euphoria of goodwill and good intentions, never doubting the sense and sensibility of their idea. Shaw's postcard must have been a rude shock, dismissed no doubt as another of his crusty rejoinders. After all, Shaw was always wrong, wasn't he? Or was he?

Of course Shaw was hardly a typical immigrant. Not for him Euston in the grey dawn, digs in West Hampstead, insecurity for a period. He had the benefit of starting at the top and working his way down. It was really not too difficult for him 'to join English Clubs' (and he derived considerable advantage therefrom). His life, however, pinpoints the unchanging dilemma of adjustment for newcomers to any society—to 'integrate' (meaningless term) and still to maintain the distinctive and valuable attributes of a different culture.

The nub of Shaw's postcard is his quite right view that the English and the Irish have each 'much to learn from their association and co-operation'. Shaw obviously feared that the Club would be 'forever Ireland' and nothing more. In this he has been proved wrong indeed. Certainly for a number of members the Club is an introspective haven saving them from the realities in England and maintaining what they sadly believe to be a reflection of life in Ireland ('times remembered'). But they are the few. The majority see the Club as a place where Shaw's idea could be realised by making the Club the point of contact between the two cultures of the two islands, and by doing that from a position of strength rather than from weakness of solo efforts. The most difficult trait of the Anglo-Saxon to accept (and to change!) is his quiet assumption of superiority, bolstered frequently by comparing the best of England with the worst of other places. The Irish Club has not been excessively chauvinistic but has endeavoured to compare like with like, to display differences for enjoyment rather than for evaluation. And in the process, members of Shaw's English Clubs have commented so frequently how much they prefer ours.

Whatever the motives for the founding of the Club, its creation nevertheless signified the emergence of an immigrant middle-class. Eaton Square, it could be said, was a long way

from the embarkation sheds in Liverpool of the Famine diaspora. The journey was precisely that of a hundred years.

1950s

It is evident that much had changed in that century in relation to the status of the Irish. Although substantially unskilled, no longer were they totally such: 22 per cent were
engaged in skilled occupations, according to the 1951 census.
Neither were they, in the dormancy of the Ulster issue, excessively nationalistic. These changes meant less concentration
by new arrivals upon the traditional areas of settlement, meant
a more diffused absorption into the general fabric of Britain.
In the early fifties, an increasing minority arrived with marketable skills, or with the intent of acquiring some, and shunned
the traditional ghetto areas as places of abode. One immigrant
of the fifties, now an advertising executive, told me:

Camden Town or Hammersmith were two areas of London that I determined not to live in when I came to London
in 1954. I didn't want to be identified with 'The Paddies'—
I knew all about them before leaving Ireland. Anyway, what
was the point of coming to London, unless one met and got
to know English people. Mind you, I spent my first few
weeks feeling pretty miserable in a room in Earls Court.
But I gradually got to know people—Earls Court was like a
village then—and began to have fun. I didn't find any prejudice regarding a job, answering an advertisement in the
London *Evening Standard* landed me into the production
department of an advertising agency, where I operated a
Gestetner duplicating machine for which I was paid eight
pounds a week. That was fantastic money to me, then—at
least twice what I would have earned in Ireland, and then
only if I knew someone with a bit of 'pull' to get me ap-
prenticed to a solicitor or something like that.

Anyway, here I was at twenty-two with my own flat and
spending money; I had about four pounds to spend on myself ... or on girls, as it turned out. I had a fantastic time
with the girls at work, you know what English girls are

like ... compared to Irish girls. Although I felt a bit guilty at first, you know being a Catholic, I thought 'when in Rome ...', what's the point of being in England unless one enjoys it. So in a few months I had gone through half the girls in the place and got a bit bored and concentrated on the job. And then I ran up against my first bit of prejudice —this supervisor started making anti-Irish cracks, about the ports in the war and drunken Paddies and that sort of thing. But you know, he only started that when I began to point out his mistakes to him in the print-room! That's how cocky I was then. So I moved to another agency as production manager, where there was an even more interesting crop of girls, though now I was beginning to get a bit selective, wanting something on top as well, you know. Of course, I went to Ireland on holiday every year, but I was always damn glad to come back here and the fellows I grew up with who hadn't left seemed terribly dull, really stuck in a mediocre rut. Then at the advertising agency they made me a junior executive, so I started watching my 'P's and Q's' then; I used to wear a stiff white collar and I brushed-up my table manners, learned about wines and all that rubbish—and it paid off. They made me an account executive. So why should I have lived in Camden Town or some Irish place? Mind you, my one true friend is Irish, and even many of my other friends are either of Irish descent, or have an Irish temperament. I'm not sensitive about my nationality, although nowadays some people don't take me as Irish; I'm not sensitive about phrases like 'bloody Irish at it again' which is what one sometimes hears about the North from people I do business with. After all, it's my job not to be offended.

My informant, now the possessor of an elegant London apartment and a boat on the South Coast, represents the small but increasing proportion who came in the fifties, and were intent on not just mere survival but on positively exploiting the novel territories of their social, cultural, and intellectual expansion in Britain. Cracks began to appear in the old mould of lumpen proletarian immigration at different levels. By contrast with the previous decades, immigrant girls began to move away from domestic service and to receive training as nurses, and to a lesser extent as teachers. Men who in previous decades were content to remain as navvies now sought opportunities to become sub-contractors. Barmen served with an eye to the day when they might become landlord of their own premises. Greater numbers of both sexes were to be found in white-collar employment, attending evening classes in search of marketable credentials, and residing in middle-class districts. Higher and more widespread education in Ireland gave rise to new initiative which grafted on to the old émigré tradition a more positive approach to life in the new country. A pointer to future possibilities was provided by the town of Southampton when, in 1955, it elected as Mayor a Dubliner, Mollie O'Higgins, who had come to work as a 'clippie' on the buses in the First World War. In London an Irish employment agency was founded specializing in hotel and catering staff; some of those who first came on its books were subsequently to open their own hotels and restaurants. There were even some who came strictly on business: McConnell's Advertising Agency of Dublin, whose chairman had been one of the founders of the Eaton Square Irish Club, expanded to Britain with branches in London and other cities. Eamonn Andrews, a young boxing commentator on Radio Eireann, was invited to audition for the B.B.C. and stayed on to chair the top-rating show of the time, 'What's My Line'. Other, less dramatic, examples came to work in publishing and journalism, in banks and insurance offices.

One family made notable impact: Dominic Behan was working in the fifties as a housepainter by day and writing scripts in the evening for the B.B.C. where the poet Louis MacNeice and other expatriate Irish literati were enjoying something of a golden vein, inheritors of the tradition of Irish émigré literary entertainment. His brother Brendan's play *The Hostage* was, in the critic Kenneth Tynan's observation, 'an example of Ireland's function every twenty years or so to provide a playwright who will kick English drama from the past into the present'. Much of Brendan Behan's literary career irretrievably connected with the strands of emigration;

the playwright who was now feted by the literary aristocracy had, as we have seen, been a Borstal Boy for I.R.A. offences in Liverpool. While Brendan and Dominic fulfilled one tradition, a third brother, Brian, fulfilled another immigrant inheritance, that of Feargus O'Connor's Republican Socialism or, as it was more popularly known then in the fifties, 'left-wing agitation', which reflected the further diffusion of immigrant impact at an elementary level. The strike on London's South Bank in 1958 may be regarded as evidence of that trend.

The post-war building boom in Britain had continued into the fifties, notably with the construction of massive office blocks and commercial buildings, such as the Shell Building and the South Bank concrete complex. At least half the work forces on these massive sites were Irish; emigration from Ireland, in spite of social advances, was still running at upward of 40,000 per year. The labouring men from the rural areas of Connacht found work mainly on the building sites of the London South Bank and lived in the near-by Elephant and Castle slum districts, where it was not uncommon to hear Connemara Gaelic spoken in the public houses. The work was rough and tough, particularly in the pile-boring and in the excavation of the huge basins to take thousands of tons of liquid cement which today form the concrete foundations of the impressive building achievement. In Behan's effusive recollection:

Round the edge of the crater the draglines lifted their iron necks and sent their teeth darting down like a great buzzard's beak. Remorselessly they tore at the ground and deeper and deeper grew the cavity ... then into it climbed the carpenters and steel-fixers; on platforms ninety feet below ground they shored-up the avenging clay with struts of timber and steel. Then from a swan-like crane, with its rider perched one hundred and fifty feet up, came an endless golden, thick creamy porridge that will set rock-hard to carry the monster building on its back.[5]

[5] Brian Behan, *With Breast Expanded*, London: MacGibbon & Kee, 1964.

Such classical endeavour, to Brian Behan's radical political instincts, merely highlighted the hazards involved in the creation of 'capitalistic monuments' and seemed incongruous with the work and living conditions of those who laboured in their construction. Behan records: 'Four men died before that silly roof was stuck on, like a clown's hat atop a bear's head ... the men know that even if the firm is blameless it is always their own kind who lie crushed and mangled beneath the planner's beams.' Many a novice complainer in an Irish work gang, as Brian Behan remembers, 'was shut up with a belt across the face by an Irish foreman intent only on bonus profit for himself'. The system of individual work-gang bonuses which encouraged such bullying was but one of the work conditions which Behan campaigned against. As a former member of a turf-cutting gang in, literally, the bogs of Ireland (where he had earned thirty shillings a week before emigrating), Behan was particularly sensitive to 'the evils of pitting worker against worker'. He became active as a strike-leader and his colourful turn of militant invective found support from among a minority of the Irish workforce. Some of his strongest supporters were drawn from the ranks of the clannish Connemara men, from Scots-Irish adherents of Keir Hardie who were instrumental in mounting a lock-out strike on the South Bank site, 'with the biggest ring-a-rosy picket on a building site the industry has ever witnessed', which culminated in a pitched battle with the police. Brian Behan served a prison sentence for 'Incitement to riot', and was subsequently black-listed from sites by unions and employers alike.

The significance of the South Bank strike in Irish terms was that it characterized the 'diffusion' of the fifties, i.e. the moving out from the straitjacketed immigrant mentality of regarding themselves as mere economic fodder with no function other than that of a passive work-force. The trade union militancy of Irish workers was in part the product of disillusion with the administration in Ireland which had failed to provide employment in Ireland. All through the fifties the surplus of unemployed rarely fell below 40,000 a year and the 'dole' offered the magnificent weekly sum of thirty-four shillings. Many of the young men who left in that decade carried with them a political bitterness against their own native establishment which was to find expression in their lives in Britain, most notably in trade union involvement. Even for the soft under-belly of migrant construction workers, conditions and wages had enormously improved, partly due to the large-scale site strikes. But the most notable change in the pattern of the fifties lay with the diffusion of a previous near-total labouring force into more varied and improved employment. Accompanying this improvement was a noticeable lessening of anti-British feeling, a potent confirmation of change. This was noted with some alarm in a confidential report of the Anti-Partition League in 1957. (The League had been active in Britain in the earlier years of the decade, attempting to mobilize the 850,000 Irish to influence the Ulster question as an electoral issue and was in receipt of a secret subvention from the Irish Government.) But in a decade of ostensible political peace between both countries membership had dwindled; discussing the causes of lapse of support, the national organizer Tadhg Feehan noted:

A potentially influential number of Irish comprising the professional class or those doing well in business, are primarily concerned with securing a good social standing in their particular milieu. They remain, of course, Irish in most senses of the term and are quite happy to be identified with Irish functions of a social character. But they are not prepared either to take active steps in relation to partition or to be, at least publicly, identified with direct efforts to end it through action in this country. A second category which comprises the vast bulk of the Irish-born population, consists of those who are engaged in subordinate employment. Their primary concern is to make a living and, if possible, put some money aside. Indeed one hears stories, from priests and others with considerable experience of our compatriots in this country, of a striking absence of national sentiment in great numbers of the Irish-born population and particularly in the more recent and younger immigrants.

The 'striking absence of national sentiment' may have been

no more than more pragmatic attitudes of those who came in
the late fifties, and who were more intent on investigating
and exploiting the new opportunities in Britain. Tricolour
flag-waving and lip-service to the sacred cows of the Republic
after all, had not provided them with the means to earn a
living there, and many of the younger immigrants were im
patient with such rhetoric. Indeed, for some Ireland was a dull
place, depleted of manpower and initiative and appearing to
offer little future challenge, whereas Britain by contrast offered
work and, for many, the excitement of new terrain. It was an
attitude of new positivism, characterized by a diffusion into
more ambitious areas of employment and living and which
was to produce in the sixties a more independent community.

PART II

THE IRISH NOW

The Irish Now

The decade of 1960–70, marking the end of a century of relentless Irish immigration to Britain, marked also the beginning of a decade more fruitful for the Irish than any other
time in the previous century's diaspora. The 'new positivism'
of many of the Irish during this period was due mainly to
increased levels of education and living standards in Ireland
and encouraged them—against a background of political peace
between both countries—to involve themselves more produc-
tively in the life of their adopted country.

Many factors combined to encourage their enhanced status,
not least the radical changes in Britain during the sixties which
dovetailed with the improved changes in the Irish. The falling-
away from imperial attitudes in Britain was reflected in politics,
in the media, and in the country at large, with an accelerated
closing of the gap in earning-power between the working- and
middle-classes. In politics, the speech of Conservative Prime
Minister Harold Macmillan on 'The Winds of Change' (delivered in South Africa with the tired, if prudent, air of one
who fears the spectacle of restless servants brandishing kitchen
knives in the drawing-room) affirmed the growing inevitability
of colonial disintegration. In the media, a similar internal disintegration was voiced in the emergence of the so-called
'kitchen-sink' writers such as John Osborne, Alan Sillitoe,
Shelagh Delaney *et al.*, now trenchantly demanding that the
plaintiff voice of the kitchen be heard in the drawing-room.

These writers allied themselves with the burgeoning 'meritocracy' which revived the Labour Party in the early sixties,
articulating as they did the strident voice of those who took
pride in being working-class (or variations thereof) and who
now asked to occupy the recesses of power formerly the sanc-
tum of the traditionally better-off.

And the Irish, by now an equally burgeoning 'meritocracy'
(though formerly the most hidebound of the habitués of
Britain's kitchens) found that the egalitarian changes provided

ideal cover from which to move tentatively out and upwards into the opportunistic sixties. As an immigrant people in the Britain of the sixties they were less subject to hostility, and more the object of tolerance—if not affection—than at any time in the long history of their diaspora to Britain. How they reacted to that radically-changed circumstance is the scope of the remainder of this book.

In Politics

A rough beast ... slouches toward Bethlehem to be born
—William Butler Yeats

One of the most immediate effects of the upgrading of the Irish community in the sixties was to be perceived in the political arena. Their new social solidity encouraged the emergence of a political involvement in domestic British politics: by the sixties almost every major local authority had Irish-born representation. This was most strong in the traditional immigrant areas, but in the less obvious districts the Irish who were members of the Labour Party were encouraged to stand for election, an important factor being the personal encouragement provided by first and second generation Irish, now more secure in their own integrated identity and happily free of the pressure of the 'Irish Question' which had deflected loyalties previously.[1]

Accordingly, when Irish candidates went forward at local elections in the sixties, their interests were not to do with the 'Irish Question' (then dormant) but rather with local issues of housing, education, amenities, and such. Many indeed played down their Irishness and campaigned on matters of broad party policy. For most Irish candidates there was no conscious 'Irish Vote' to woo, except for those wishing to represent areas of traditional immigration, and here the Irish vote was coupled more to issues of specific interest such as schools, with an absence of overt Catholic pressure. There was little electoral guidance from church pulpits; one priest in a Middlesbrough ward saw the distinction as: 'Taking our religion from Rome, but our politics from our bellies.' This gut reaction was more Irish than Catholic, in the sense that the mass of the Irish immigrants were, in British terms, working-class voters. Their

[1] Of the 363 Labour Members of Parliament who formed the majority in the House of Commons from 1966–70, around 35 were of immigrant Irish descent.

natural antipathy to 'the gentry' of the Conservative Party was compounded by the links which that party maintained with the Unionist Government of Northern Ireland. Though the middle-classes of the Irish in Britain tended to vote Conservative, the majority of the immigrants who exercised the vote were loyal to the Labour Party even when they moved marginally up the socio-economic scale.

This traditional loyalty was given a tremendous boost by the return to power of Labour administration in 1964 and by the subsequent activities of a Cabinet in which the names of Healey, Brown, and Callaghan invoked secure echoes in Irish pubs and clubs all over Britain. And not only did that 'holy trinity' make much and effective use of their Irish ancestry in public speeches, but the administration which they strongly influenced helped bring about a rapport between the Governments of Ireland and England unequalled in recent history. The highlights of this rapport were: (a) the payment by the British authorities of pensions and other social security benefits to workers returned to Ireland (who were formerly domiciled in Britain). (b) The signing of the Anglo-Irish Free Trade Agreement, which provided for wider trade between both countries. (c) The return to Irish soil of 'patriot' remains, notably those of Sir Roger Casement: mystic, adventurer, and ex-colonial civil servant. Casement had been hanged as a traitor fifty years earlier, on a charge of running guns to Ireland to aid the rebels of the Republic declared in 1916. It is a telling commentary on the contrasting historical perspectives of the Irish *vis-à-vis* the English that the name Casement would draw a blank from most British, while invoking among Irish revered memories of a martyred patriot. The remains of Barnes and McCormick, executed in connection with the I.R.A. bomb explosion in Coventry, were also returned during the Labour administration.

If politics is about people-management, then the Labour Government of the mid-to-late sixties were masters of that art in relation to the Irish in Britain. The artifice which could initiate four pop singers into the order of Member of the British Empire (largely defunct) extended to the million or so politically sullen Irish in Britain. Successive St Patrick's Day dinners at plush hotels were graced by British Cabinet Ministers proposing the toast of 'The Two Islands' and in towns and cities all over Britain, local Labour dignitaries made known their willingness to attend Irish functions. It was a high time for the emerging Irish, coming out 'from under the shadow of the still rock' and into the warm gaze of acceptance. It was a time that coincided with increased economic affluence and productivity in Ireland, and a time of similar upgrading of the Irish in Britain, who were, for instance, moving from the tenements of dilapidated areas into council housing and the suburbs. It was also a time when the economic boom in Ireland had effect upon the quality of immigrants, and consequently upon the attitude of the host community. One immediate effect of the new industrialization in Ireland was that the more criminally-prone adolescents stayed at home to work in the new factories rather than head for Coventry or Birmingham. (The police in Ireland now found themselves facing an increase in the sort of urban crime more familiar to their British counterparts.)

The media exposure of such bodies as the Irish Tourist Board and Aer Lingus also helped upgrade the image of the Irish in Britain, although their colour-supplement purveyance of deserted rural beauty produced predictable wry reaction among those driven from such uneconomic pastures, ('You can't eat the scenery'). Most pertinently of all, the sharpening focus upon the increasing coloured immigrants distracted attention away from the Irish as an alien presence. With cyclic inevitability, coloured immigrants became the object of the same hostile platitudes of 'separateness', i.e. large families, eating habits, noisy parties, that the Irish had been subject to in previous generations. It was noticeable during the early sixties the extent to which the accommodation notices in shop windows translated the slogan 'No Irish' to that of 'No Coloureds' and how that barometer of popular agitation, Speakers' Corner in London, lost its rabble of tri-colour flags and slogans to the invective of Black Power. Whereas in previous decades the issue of Northern Ireland had been a lively one at Speakers' Corner, by the mid-sixties only a handful of weary Republicans clustered around the ideal of a United Ireland.

Towards the end of the previous century the Irish vote had been profoundly affected by events in Ireland; so now in the sixties was it equally affected by a radically changed situation in Ireland.

The situation in the sixties which affected the immigrants was that the Republic was bent on economic expansion, luring in foreign industrialists with lucrative financial grants. And with some success, to the extent of slicing the British-bound emigration rate in the latter half of the sixties from around 50,000 to 25,000 annually. Britain being the principal outlet for exports, and with the new entente cordiale with the Labour administration rampant, the last thing the young go-getters of Fianna Fail wished to raise was the old spectre of 'Ulster under British Domination'. And the governing party—Fianna Fail—now led by the pragmatic Sean Lemass, perceived the patriotism of the slide-rule and financial balance sheet to be more relevant to the needs of the majority of the citizens in its care. So much so that when an Irish Cabinet Minister of the period was questioned by a journalist on the plight of Catholics in the North of Ireland, the bland reply was: 'Ah, we don't worry about them. Sure the English Catholic M.P.s at Westminster will look after them.'

The Irish Minister for Education on a St Patrick's Day visit to an Irish university graduates' club in London in 1966 urged his audience to involve themselves in the constitutional life in Britain. He told them: 'You must participate fully in the affairs of the country of your adoption. You cannot be full citizens of both countries.' His timing was impeccable, for his exhortation came at a time when the Irish in Britain had become assured and settled. They were moving out from the ghetto mentality, making inroads into the mainstream of national life, buying pubs and founding construction firms, leaving the decaying city centres for the suburbs. They were the largest single ethnic group in Britain and slowly and reluctantly they were beginning to realize that for most of them there would be no 'going home next year'; that they were here to stay.

One obvious corollary was political involvement, initially at local level, and in 1969 came the culmination of this 'infiltration', with the election of Mr Michael O'Halloran as Member of Parliament for the London constituency of Islington North. His election is of importance, for he is a man very much of his own émigré people. He owed his candidature not only to his long-standing service on Islington Council, but in some measure also to the influence of the Irish in the local Labour Party selection committee, and to that lobby's determination that 'it was about time we had one of our own in the House'. In demeanour and personality O'Halloran is representative of the broad mass of Irish immigrants to Britain, having modest formal education, and having retained, after twenty years, his unmistakable accent. His election is significant, for it marks the breakthrough of the Irish immigrant into the constitutional life of the nation and the acceptance of that community by the establishment.

Most pertinent of all, O'Halloran's election to Westminster —for centuries a bane in the minds of the Irish—provided impetus for almost a million Irish-born to vote for candidates in the 1970 General Election. According to a survey published in the *Irish Post* after the election, 84 per cent of the 'Irish vote' had been cast in favour of Labour Party candidates. It is worth relating that assertion to the contemporary awareness of the Ethnic vote.

THE IRISH 'ETHNIC VOTE' has been largely underestimated by British political parties. The Labour Party had been marginally more conscious of the possibilities of the Irish vote for a variety of reasons; not least of these being the prominence of Irish-born and 'Brit-Irish' personalities in a number of powerful trade unions. In the run-up to the Election of 1970, both parties became aware of the Irish vote through the storm-clouds of the Ulster issue and its effects upon Irish voters in Britain. In the run-up to that election, the twenty-five constituencies with potentially decisive Irish voting power were:

Constituency		*Irish Percentage of Population*
Willesden East	– London	14·5
Hammersmith	– London	10·9

Constituency		*Irish Percentage of Population*
Ardwick	– Manchester	10·1
Willesden West	– London	10·0
Kensington North	– London	9·6
Islington North	– London	9·5
Paddington North	– London	9·3
Gorbals	– Glasgow	9·2
Barons Court	– London	9·0
Sparkbrook	– Birmingham	8·7
St Pancras North	– London	8·6
Paddington South	– London	8·5
Moss Side	– Manchester	8·1
Ladywood	– Birmingham	7·9
Small Heath	– Birmingham	7·6
Coventry South	– Coventry	7·6
Acton	– London	7·3
Hampstead	– London	7·3
Selly Oak	– Birmingham	7·1
Handsworth	– Birmingham	6·9
Holborn/ St Pancras	– London	6·8
All Saints	– Birmingham	6·7
Exchange	– Manchester	6·6
Islington East	– London	6·5
Coventry North	– Coventry	6·5

Source: Shelley Markham, *What About the Irish?*, London: Runnymede Trust, 1971.

In the General Election, 18 June 1970, a Conservative Government was returned on a national voting swing of *4·7 per cent*. Even allowing for a margin of 'variables' due to re-housing and other demographic changes since 1966, it is clear that most of the above constituencies could have been heavily influenced by the Irish vote. In the event, and in the face of a national voting swing towards Conservative candidates of 4·7 per cent, *twenty of the above twenty-five* constituencies returned a *Labour* candidate. (In at least two of the constituencies which returned a *Conservative* candidate, the members had strong personal rapport with the Irish in the constituency.)

It would be rash to conclude that, of those twenty-five named constituencies with the highest Irish percentage of voters, the twenty who returned Labour candidates did so *critically* on the Irish vote. But in the light of other circumstantial evidence, it is clear that the Irish ethnic vote can no longer be disregarded. In two Birmingham constituencies, for example, the Conservative members hold their seats on a swing of less than 2 per cent, yet the Irish-born form 7 per cent of each constituency's electorate. In their work *The British General Election, 1970,* the authors David Butler and Michael Pinto-Duschinsky decided that three seats in the South-East were definitely decided by the Irish vote, while the political colouring of another five seats possibly resided with the Irish. Even with the recent re-drawing of constituency boundaries, around thirty parliamentary seats could be decided by the *en bloc* Irish vote. Given that Irish-born form around 2 per cent of the population, and that those thirty seats represent around 5 per cent of the total allocation, it would appear that the immigrants form a potential electoral power disproportionate to their numbers. This is one of the unforeseen advantages of the ghetto-grouping, proving a belated pay-off for the miseries of the nineteenth-century slum settlements, and the tradition bred therefrom.

What is notably different from the political attitudes of those settlements is the relative absence of clerical influence in relation to current Irish voting attitudes on domestic British issues. Except in the case of the Ulster issue, Irish priests display but minimum interest and influence in relation to the party political attitudes of their compatriots. Even such a potentially emotive issue as the Abortion Act of 1967, by which a Labour administration legalized surgical pregnancy terminations, did not arouse any meaningful Irish Catholic lobby in electoral terms. It is true that various Catholic lobbies opposed the measure, lobbies such as the Union of Catholic Mothers, but these were representative of general Catholic attitudes rather than of specific immigrant interest. The

Birmingham constituency of Perry Barr provides a case in point.

Prior to the General Election of 1970, the Labour Party incumbent was Christopher Price, who had supported the movement for Abortion Law Reform. In the year prior to the Election, his Conservative opponent Joseph Kinsey had formulated a rapport with influential sections of the Birmingham-Irish community and had been instrumental in securing the lease of a local hall for use as Irish club premises. Remembering that the Irish generally voted Labour, the Conservative Kinsey was returned on a swing of 12·6 per cent; and local observers judge him to have netted most of the available Irish vote, not so much as a reaction to the Labour candidate's identity with the Abortion Bill, but more because of his sympathetic assistance to the Irish community on practical welfare matters. There are other such examples which suggest that the Irish vote is not heavily vulnerable to issues of abstract Catholic morality, but is subject rather to a straight functional influence of a candidate's rapport with the Irish community, and what that community feels it may tangibly receive in return for its vote! The Irish in Britain are historically conditioned towards a pragmatic use of their vote, a reaction originating in the parish-pump 'you scratch my back: I'll scratch yours' level of politics in Ireland.

They are not susceptible, generally speaking, to appeals of broad or abstract philosophical difference. They have traditionally voted Labour because that party traditionally reflected what the Irish deemed to be most close to their own material interests in Britain. It was under cautious Labour Party encouragement that they have emerged as a present-day influential—and potentially weighty—factor in the political life of their adopted country. Not the least significant implication of that 'slouching towards Bethlehem to be born' political emergence is the pointer towards future political participation of other ethnic minorities. At the local elections of May 1971, for instance, over 150 Irish candidates presented themselves to the electorate; a hundred more than the previous time. Three-quarters of them stood for Labour. In Michael O'Halloran's constituency of Islington North, six Irish-born candidates were elected. In Luton another six of the forty-eight-member council were Irish-born. By the early 1970s the Irish occupied the office of Mayor in three British boroughs —Luton, Derby, and Kettering. A look at one of these personalities, the Mayor of Luton, is relevant, for like O'Halloran, he epitomizes the upward movement of the Irish.

James Cussen, fifty-year-old Mayor of Luton, emigrant from Limerick, is now a comfortable partner in a Luton building firm. It wasn't always like that. For James Cussen, emigrant, came to England in 1939, a time of severe economic depression in Ireland. He was just one of a batch of migrant workers who crossed the Irish Sea and—this being wartime—were directed to whatever strategic area in which labour was required. He was sent to Northampton, to help build an air-field. As he remembers it: 'We were billeted in a nissen hut, all Irish lads just over. When the air-raid warning went we thought we were being bombed. We had no training in this sort of thing, so we made like the clappers for the door and ran out all over the fields. And some must have kept running, for there were a few missing the following morning.'

From that first introduction to Britain, coming down in the blacked-out train from the entry port of Holyhead and working on the aerodrome, Cussen went to Luton to look for 'digs' in one of the many 'Irish Houses' in the area. He found work in a local factory, walked out with the landlady's daughter, and joined the local Young Socialists, 'more for the social company than the ideas. I was a raw immigrant and when someone at work said come along for a drink and a chat, I was glad to. Of course, having left Ireland at the end of the thirties when things were really bad, I had never heard of such phrases as "social justice". Mind you, I knew what social injustice meant, even if I couldn't always describe it. I knew what it meant to go to school in shoe-leather when most of my class-mates were barefoot.' His attendance at the Young Socialists gave him political ambitions, but when he went to stand as a Labour candidate after the war he ran up against an un-expected obstacle. The factory where he worked made it plain that his job rating would suffer if he were elected. Cussen remembers: 'They didn't like the idea of a worker having in-

fluence on the council, so I withdrew my application to stand.'
It is an indicative irony that, twenty-five years later, management representatives of the same Luton firm were happy to
attend the mayoral inauguration. Cussen married the landlady's
daughter, one Eve O'Connor, and at the mayoral reception he
replaced the usual string quartet with a ceili band.

The town he represents, Luton, has a population of 150,000
centred on the car industry, with an Irish colony of 15,000. In
some areas of the town, whole streets are not only Irish, but
are occupied by immigrants from particular towns in Ireland,
so that an intensely clannish air pervades these areas. To the
extent that, as one resident put it, 'If someone comes over from
the west of Ireland looking for a job, he only has to mention
what town he comes from and I'll know what street to direct
him to.'

The Irish are so ingrained in the fabric of Luton (it being
one of the stops outside London on the Great North Road
during the mass migration of the post-famine travellers) that
there was scant opposition to the prospect of an Irish mayor.
Which is in some contrast to the election of Paddy O'Connor
as Mayor of Camden some years previously (at a time when
the borough had become enlarged to include the upper middle-
class areas of Hampstead). The correspondence columns of the
local paper were the platform of a raging controversy as to
the propriety of an English borough, albeit Camden, having an
Irish mayor. Perhaps the closing comment should be that the
then Mayor of Camden, Paddy O'Connor, is the brother of the
'landlady's daughter', Eve O'Connor, who married the present
Mayor of Luton! Again, the significance of Cussen is that he
is a traditional emigrant, having come to labour and stayed on
to be mayor. And though he holidays in Ireland every year,
his roots are more with the Irish in Britain; with his family,
his church, and his community. He is part of that separate
'Middle Nation' of the Irish, and perhaps as such embraces
more of the virtues of the Irish–English than their respective
vices and has obviously been enriched by the process of
emigration.

What, it may be asked, has been the response of the other
principal British political party to the dominant support among

the Irish for the Labour Party? Until the General Election of 1970, the Conservatives were content to allow the Labour Party to make all the running with the Irish. Not that the Conservative Party was without Irish connections, particularly in the persons of Sir Toby O'Brien (an influential figure in Tory Central Office), Norman St John Stevas, M.P., and further back, former premier Harold Macmillan. But those connections were regarded, somewhat unfairly, as being with the Ascendancy (Anglo-Irish) and certainly the mass of the Irish in Britain regarded them as being far removed from themselves. The vast majority of the immigrants were and are from the southern Republic of Ireland; their natural antipathy towards Tories is compounded by the links which that party maintains with the Unionist Government of Northern Ireland, links enshrined in the official title of 'The Conservative and Unionist Party'. The extent of Irish support for Labour became a source of some concern to the hierarchy at Conservative Central Office in their intelligence operation prior to the last General Election. (During the sixties an emerging minority of Irish businessmen and new middle-class gravitated towards the Tories, mainly motivated by resentment at what was considered to be penal taxation by the Socialists. Shortly before the General Election, with the Conservative promise to return an Immigration Bill if brought to power, a particular Irish-dominated Conservative Party in the provinces made known to Central Office that if the Irish were included in the Bill there would be no cars to get the vote out on polling day.) Once the election was won, consideration of the 'Irish vote' came to fruition with the establishment of the Irish Conservative Association which has as its long-term objective, 'the improvement of communication between the Irish in Britain and the Conservative Party'. The Association has the blessing of Central Office—the powerhouse of the Tory party—and its founder is Paul Dwyer. Dwyer, a Hammersmith councillor, has all the moneyed elegance of the British upper class, allied to an acute awareness of his own Irish ancestry. It was this dichotomy, so to speak, between his socio-political position and his awareness of the traditional Labour Party hold over the immigrant Irish vote that led to his founding the Irish

Conservative Association. No one in political circles doubts that the salient long-term objective of the Association is to wean the immigrant Irish Vote away from Labour.

In its short life-span of two years, the Association has formulated the basis of what may well emerge as a significant power-structure of the Irish in Britain, simply because the formal organization exists whereby the various grass-roots interests of the Irish may be communicated to the Conservative Government of the day. It is something totally new for the rank-and-file Irish to be thus represented. Within months of its founding, the Irish Conservative Association was instrumental in handing over to a housing trust, SHAC,[2] the tenure of short-life properties in London. In the London borough of Hammersmith, it set up a community advice centre to act as go-between for the council and those in need of welfare advice.

It sees help with housing as a major contribution, a relevant priority in view of the propensity of the Irish to have, compared with other immigrant groups, the largest number of children per family. Comparisons may be odious, but if politics are often about the record of one party *vis-à-vis* another, the Association has yet to make the dramatic impact akin to the Labour Party rapport of the early sixties. Though I have it on good authority that there was an offer, via the Irish Conservative Association, that the Conservative Prime Minister, Edward Heath, would be happy to attend the annual Gaelic Games in Wembley Stadium, it is a measure of the still entrenched insularity of grass-roots Irish towards the Conservatives that *such an invitation was not forthcoming from the Irish*, and is unlikely to be until the utopia of a United Ireland is declared!

In the meantime, the Irish Conservative Association is unlikely to suffer from the absence of such dramatic declarations. The mass of the Irish in Britain are more concerned with the minutiae of day-to-day living in the country of their adop-

[2] Apt initials for Shelter Housing Advisory Centre, which revolutionized the possibility of home ownership for the poorer sections of the community and intruded upon the house monopoly of the building societies. Presently run by a Dublin priest, Father Byrne, but its activities by no means confined to the Irish. An offspring of Catholic Housing Aid Society.

tion, and it is in such areas of help with housing and welfare that the Irish Conservative Association could woo some of the immigrant Irish. That, and an increasing involvement of the Irish in Britain in the general life of the Conservative Party would appear to be the pointer for the future, for the rooted Irish in Britain, increasingly weathered in the mores of the British way of life, see parliamentary participation as the only valid way forward. As one staunch supporter of the Association said to me (himself a former Republican activist in Ireland, but now a prosperous leader of the community in Britain): 'We are here to stay. It only makes sense that we should do business with the party that for at least half of our lifetime will form the Government of Britain.'

His thinking is echoed by the growing support of a section of the Irish, mainly businessmen, for the Tories. The initiator of the movement, Paul Dwyer, has already extended this support beyond the business community, at least in terms of his own personal support. In the London local elections of May 1971, when the electorate moved massively to Labour, Dwyer held on to his Tory seat on Hammersmith Council and reckons to have been helped in this by gaining 99 per cent of the Irish vote in his ward. (It is pertinent to record, of course, that the Tory motivation in wooing the Irish is to a large extent due to the upgrading of this ethnic voting power by the Labour Party since the 1920s. This Labour encouragement was less calculated than the present Tory motivation. But such is the nature of politics.) The growth of the Irish Conservative Association, perhaps more than the election of Michael O'Halloran, signified the changed relationship of the émigrés in the sixties, marking a degree of political independence free from inherited attitudes and being specifically an offspring of a tentative affair between the Establishment and the immigrants. The Association thus became the first political casualty of the revolution in Ulster; following the Derry shootings of January 1972, the *Irish Post*, which had previously supported and publicized the efforts of the Irish Conservative Association, called for the resignation of 'those Irish people who are members of the Conservative Party'. With an about-face the paper added: 'Toryism and the Irish in Britain never had much in common—it is now repugnant that they should even breathe the same air.'

In contemplating political attitudes since the early nineteenth century, it is clear that the immigrants were swayed more by events in Ireland than in Britain. A necessary by-product of the political calm of the early sixties was the near extinction of the various organizations which had formerly campaigned for a United Ireland in the forties and fifties. Chief casualty was the Anti-Partition (Border) League which had flourished in the forties. By the late fifties its National Organizer had gone off to a comfortable sinecure in the Irish Embassy in London. The Connolly Association, under the devoted and indefatigable Desmond Greaves, continued to lobby M.P.s at Westminster, hold 'teach-ins', and published its organ of Connolly philosophy, *The Irish Democrat*. Former I.R.A. men (including some veterans of the 1939 Bombing Campaign) reminisced in pubs and gathered for meagre ritual nostalgia at Speakers' Corner in Hyde Park. Some 'bridged the gap' by joining the Labour Party. The political running of the Irish was now in the constitutional hustings of local politics. Then, in October 1968, the slumbering mad-dog of the Republican conscience awoke, prodded to life by the batons of the Royal Ulster Constabulary—and by the fortuitous presence of one television cameraman—during a Civil Rights march in Londonderry. The effects of the subsequent escalation upon the Irish here may be summarized:

1968: The Derry disturbances catalysed the dormant political consciousness. The Connolly Association stepped-up lobbying of M.P.s, followed by other organizations such as the Campaign for Democracy in Ulster, the United Ireland Association, and other minority groupings.

1969: The establishment of a British section of the Northern Ireland Civil Rights Association which attempted to unify the disparate organizations under a 'Civil Rights' umbrella with some success. But the attacks upon Belfast Catholic enclaves stimulated more individualistic reaction. Eamon Smullen, a trade union official and Republican Socialist, was sentenced to a term of imprisonment following an alleged attempt to purchase arms in Huddersfield. Collections were made on building sites and funds remitted to Catholic areas of Derry and Belfast. The split in the Republican Movement in Ireland was reflected in a similar division among Republicans in Britain into the camps of the Provisional and Official I.R.A. As the sparsely-attended Hyde Park gatherings of the sixties swelled visibly against the flaring emotions of Northern Ireland, the ragged straggle of marchers to Trafalgar Square took on a new vigour. (One of the more bizarre aspects of Republican marches in Britain is to hear a visiting Republican leader from Dublin vehemently denounce Westminster under the impassive protection of the London Metropolitan Police. And then, without geographic accuracy, I have seen the President of Sinn Féin, standing in Trafalgar Square with his back to Westminster, point an accusing political finger at, in effect, the National Gallery!) Some incensed and footloose young men returned to man the barricades in the Catholic enclaves. Both the Ulster Office and the Irish Embassy became the target of demonstrations, but the great mass of the Irish immigrants remained outwardly quiescent.

1970: Increased Ulster warfare produced attendant militancy in Britain. In July a C.S. gas canister was tossed into the debating chamber of the House of Commons and a twenty-seven-year-old native of Wexford, James Anthony Roche, was subsequently sentenced to eighteen months' imprisonment. In the following month of August, Special Branch Officers raided a house in Tooting, South London, and uncovered what was later alleged to be an I.R.A. bomb-making cell. Grim echoes of the Bombing Campaign of 1939 were evoked by headlines in the mass-circulation newspapers, a recall made more potent by an explosion a short time later of a bomb being taken from a London cinema. At the trial of the Tooting men, however, it was stated by the leader of the group, Brendan Magill, that no repetition of the war bombing had been envisaged by the I.R.A. group of which he was a self-confessed officer. Police evidence, on the other hand, asserted that the materials found were for use against the C.S. factory at Dorking, Surrey.

In contrast to previous convictions of I.R.A. men in Britain, Magill was fortunate in receiving a comparatively light sentence of two years. Magill, thirty-seven at the time of his conviction and a family man with an English wife and five children, was the owner of a prosperous antique furniture business. He had lived a law-abiding life in Britain for fifteen years until the trauma of his native Northern Ireland awoke a Republicanism that was to land him in the dock.

The man who startled the Commons with a spluttering of C.S. gas, James Roche, was similarly moved to action by events in Ulster. A member of the Marxist-orientated Irish Solidarity Campaign which is entirely a British-based organization, Roche had made two unsuccessful attempts to complete a university graduation but had been frustrated by a combination of personal impatience and lack of funds. He had worked in factories in London where his political sense had involved him in trade-union agitation and in the months preceding the House of Commons incident he had been on the barricades in Derry with Bernadette Devlin. Apart from the incident in Parliament, he is pinned into historical fabric by his very name, Roche; the Irish provincial town in which he was born has long been dominated by the Roche Castle of the Norman Conquest of Henry II, the conquest which marked the original British presence in Ireland.

For those who like to perceive such historical undercurrents, the organization of which he is an active leader, the Irish Solidarity Campaign, consists of an almost even split between English student socialists, left-wingers, and Irish students in Britain. Roche's parliamentary debut, in fact, served as an effective blast upon the organization's recruiting trumpet, with the *Guardian* newspaper account of the incident subsequently becoming a party-piece in British left-wing university circles. It is heard to best effect when delivered with a *sotto voce* emphasis upon the italicized phrases (my italics, not the *Guardian*'s).

'Any panic which the 100 M.P.s present might have felt was swamped by their total disbelief. During the 30 seconds between the throwing of the canister and the rising of the smoke only Mr Andrew Faulds, Labour M.P. for Smethwick and traditionally the noisiest member of the House, got up. Mr Tom Swain, Labour M.P. for Derbyshire North-East, who was sitting near him on the front bench below the gangway, tried to stamp out the smouldering canister, but he was overcome by smoke. Mr Swain, aged 58, who has already suffered a serious heart attack this year, was later taken to Westminster Hospital.

'(The Speaker, Dr Horace King, was seen from farther along the gallery to have collapsed in his chair. Sir Robert Grant-Ferris, Deputy Speaker, said later: "I grabbed him by both arms, pulled him from the chair, and assisted him out of the back of the Chamber.")

'Soon the smoke had risen to the level of the front benches —and the smell of the Bogside and stinging, unreal tears came to all our eyes.

'Mr Anthony Barber cut short his statement on the Common Market and *left the Chamber quickly*.

'Mr Robert Carr who had just made a statement on the future of the Prices and Incomes Board, crouched beneath the dispatch box *with his parliamentary secretary, Mr Dudley Smith*.

'Mrs Barbara Castle who a few minutes earlier had accused Mr Carr of personal and political vindictiveness, fled from the Chamber *without her handbag*.

'She was followed by her front-bench colleagues: Mr George Thomson who was about to answer the Common Market statement; Mr Fred Peart, former Leader of the House; and Mr Mellish, Opposition Chief Whip, who had been only a few inches from the second canister. Later Mr Mellish said: "It was right under my feet, the first one. I thought it was a hand grenade. I ran. I went like a bomb. *I wasn't going to read my bloody obituary in The Times*."

'... The Speaker's bewigged clerks brought up the rear muttering: "*Sitting suspended*."

'Mr John Biggs-Davidson (C. Chigwell) said afterwards that he and the Serjeant-at-Arms had gone towards the canister to stamp it out. "I tried to approach it but got lost in gas. My face was burning, my eyes running, and I was retching—and out I went."

'The Chamber was uninhabitable for two hours and when M.P.s came back coughing at 6.30 p.m. they were forced to hold handkerchiefs over their faces.

'Meanwhile, in the police room which overlooks New Palace Yard, the man was being questioned by the Attorney-General, Sir Peter Rawlinson. Eventually, without his shirt but wearing a jacket, he was bundled into a police van bound for Cannon Row. He was accompanied by a wastepaper basket containing the two burnt out canisters.

'Back in the Commons, the Speaker announced: "I have to inform the House that the man who caused the disturbance was taken into custody by the Serjeant-at-Arms, and I have directed that he be given into custody of the civil police."

'Mr Barber got up and started his statement again. But this time the public gallery was closed. The burn on the carpet a few inches from where he stood and the smarting eyes of his colleagues were the only evidence that *something strange had happened.*[3]

By the end of 1970, the worsening Ulster situation had produced in Britain no less than a dozen political organizations, representing an equal disparity of political attitude. The partly-successful effort of the previous year by the London Executive of the Northern Ireland Civil Rights Association to unite these elements now collapsed under the weight of individual passions. It may be worth recording the organizations which attempt to 'politicize' the Irish in Britain in relation to Ulster.

The Connolly Association, in existence since the 1930s. Though its purveying of Connolly Socialism had earned it the alarmist odium of parish priests in Ireland—'a front for Communism'—the Association alone upheld a doctrine of concerned political involvement with the immigrants. Probably the most influential of all the organizations, in the context of long-term political influence.

United Ireland Association is a descendant of the Anti-Partition League of the 1940s; mainly composed of middle-

[3] From a report by Christine Eade in the *Guardian* of 24 July 1970.

aged, middle-class members it has provided a comfortable outlet over the generations for immigrant emotional indulgence in the idea of a United Ireland.

Irish Republican Army, interestingly enough, is not an illegal organization in Britain. The British wing followed the ideological division of 1969 into 'Provisionals' and 'Officials'. The latter section in Britain tends to attract the more politically educated and thoughtful, with a broadly-based political attitude towards Ulster. By contrast the Provisionals purvey a more simplistic solution of military strategy, but the hard core of both groups in Britain consist of trained veterans of previous guerilla campaigns in Ireland. Brendan Magill, arrested in Tooting, South London, in 1970 was, at the time of his conviction, chief of the British-based Provisional I.R.A. Both organizations hardly command two hundred members nationwide—a minute proportion of the one million Irish-born in Britain.

Irish Solidarity Campaign is a Marxist-oriented grouping of Irish and British members. At the time of writing, joint leaders are Bernadette Devlin and James Roche of C.S. gas note. A march in Glasgow organized in September 1971 by I.S.C. resulted in sectarian violence, during which a police inspector was slashed with that traditional Glasgow weapon, the open razor. Again, the organization hardly numbers more than 200 active members, nationwide.

Irish National Liberation Solidarity Front is the creation of one Edward Davoren, a young veteran of student protest at the London School of Economics. Following a Maoist line of analysis, and harking on the slogan: 'Political power comes out of the barrel of a gun', the organization is noted for the violence of its slogans and speeches, not least in its liberal use of the transatlantic impact of the term 'pig' to denote policemen. Apart from the Ulster issue it has attempted to capitalize on what it terms 'police harassment of working-class people'—without success. Total national support hardly exceeds 200.

Campaign for Social Justice in Northern Island, by contrast with the preceding London-based movements, is mainly active in Birmingham where, during 1970, it held meetings and marches at the rate of one a month. Maintaining a wide cross-section of support from among immigrants in Birmingham, its activities were somewhat limited following the imprisonment of its organizer, Tom McDowell, in Ulster during 1971.

Campaign for Democracy in Ulster works entirely with the parliamentary lobby and reflects the traditional alignment of British left-wing Labour thinking with Irish self-determination. Activists include Paul Rose, Labour M.P. for a Manchester constituency. Its political platform is one of 'Democracy in Ulster', rather than abolition of the Border.

These were the organizations which, during 1970, in Britain the 'umbrella' Northern Ireland Civil Rights Association attempted to blend into a cohesive force. In the Irish tradition of acrimony, it failed. In terms of impact upon the Irish community generally, the significant observation is that the total number of active followers of the above combined organizations do not exceed twenty-five thousand, or $2\frac{1}{2}$ per cent of the total immigrant Irish community.

1971: Any survey of that year of bitter sectarian bloodshed in Northern Ireland must distinguish between the pre-Internment and post-Internment periods. Pre-Internment effects upon the Irish in Britain were to be perceived at various levels. Among the 'politicized', i.e. those members of the previously-listed organizations, the routine of meetings continued with be-flagged and ragged processions of Irish protesters almost every weekend in London and Birmingham. Fleet Street newspaper editors became resigned to extra mail deliveries of irate letters from correspondents with Irish-sounding names, proposing a wide variety of conflicting solutions. In 'Irish' pubs and clubs, collections for the I.R.A. met with generous response. Bernadette Devlin, though pregnant with impending out-of-wedlock child, was fêted at meetings, and, remembering Parnell, that reaction at least marked a departure from traditional attitudes.

Traditional attitudes, however, were maintained by the petty bickering that existed between the various organizations. The introduction of Internment by the Ulster Government on 13 August 1971—incurring detention of hundreds of 'suspects' —and the scope of the backlash provided the émigré organizations with some measure of agreement. The subsequent formation of the Anti-Internment League in Britain allowed many of the bodies at least to co-operate in being united against the Internment measures. Internment also produced another side-effect of minor interest. Student opinion at English universities became polarized along the lines of the Suez differences of 1956. At one of the largest immigrant demonstrations in 1971 it was notable that half the marchers were made up of contingents of International Socialists from the various universities, forming a rare alliance of British intelligentsia and immigrant Irish, and providing a hark-back to the demonstrations of the 1920s in protest against Government policy in Ireland at the time.

A more dramatic hark-back to the twenties was an explosion in London on the morning of the march, 31 October, when a charge of plastic blasted a floor of the prestige 600 ft Post Office Tower and sent tons of masonry and steel tumbling through the early-morning quietude of Central London. The following day's newspapers were unanimous in assuming I.R.A. responsibility; an assumption encouraged by the anonymous joker who rang the Press Association and declared the explosion to be 'the work of the Kilburn (London) battalion of the I.R.A.'. Curiously enough, none of the known members of the I.R.A. who stewarded the march later that day were questioned by the authorities. Nevertheless, the incident incurred a week of scare-mongering and unearthed the inevitable crop of hoaxers.

The Irish community generally reacted to the explosion in terms of neighbours' reactions—which were tolerant. That good natured tolerance was to severely diminish during the months following Internment, directly affected by the deaths of British soldiers in Ulster. The Internment policy of the Ulster Government, which had been successful in the twenties, thirties, and fifties in containing 'the enemy within the gates', now produced running gun-battles on the streets of Belfast. Following the fateful 13 August 1971, each successive week witnessed the death of a soldier in Ulster and a consequent hardening of attitude in Britain towards 'the Oirish'. There was no overt antagonism on the scale of the 1920s; rather a series of isolated instances: The State Theatre in London's

Kilburn, an area of heavy Irish concentration, refused to accept the traditional St Patrick's Day Concert for 1972. The theatre owners, the Rank Organization, claimed bomb-threat fears and other political considerations. English Catholic parishioners complained to their priests concerning collections outside church doors for Republican funds. A Tipperary-born priest, Father Michael Connolly, serving in a Wolverhampton parish, was taken to task by Enoch Powell M.P., over a newspaper report of remarks allegedly made by the priest at an I.R.A. meeting in Dublin. In South London, an Irishwoman who had collected for Ulster refugees in 1970 (her neighbours had generously donated) received in this soldier-killing latter half of 1971 a predictably hostile reaction from neighbours.

Stronger reaction was provoked by the events in Londonderry of January 1972, when soldiers of the Parachute Brigade advanced into the Bogside area of the city—held by the I.R.A. —and thirteen civilians died under fire. In the ensuing spate of charge and counter-charge, British hostility towards the Irish reached a new pitch; the Irish generally believing the civilians to have been murdered while most of the British public remained convinced that the soldiers had first been fired upon.

For the Irish, all the inherited ghostly victims of history were revived in emotional hysteria, culminating with the burning of the British Embassy in Dublin ... which produced a backlash of hostility towards the immigrants in Britain. Offices of Irish businesses were inundated with telephonic exhortations to 'go home, Paddy' and at more vulnerable levels of employment, Irish secretaries and white-collar workers faced sudden refusals of employment. This hostility was heightened some weeks later when an I.R.A. retaliatory explosion at the Aldershot, Hampshire barracks of the Parachute Brigade snuffed out the lives, not of soldiers, but of five women cleaners, a priest, and a gardener. The explosion, comparable to the Fenian dynamiting of Clerkenwell Prison which had claimed a dozen innocent lives a century previous, left a residue of hostility likely to linger for some time.

An immediate reaction to the Aldershot deaths was a slump in demand for branded Irish goods, with one supermarket chain in London clearing its shelves of Irish produce, while in the Midlands a large accountancy firm instructed its branches to divest themselves of Irish clients. There were some sporadic incidents in public houses and in one such flare-up in the Holloway district of London knives were used in a running fracas between Irish and West Indian protagonists. In Luton, a town with a substantial Irish population, a man collecting for the dependants of internees in Northern Ireland had his garage set on fire.

These were some of the outward manifestations of an impatient British public, increasingly affected by the murderous turn of events in Ulster. At a less dramatic level there followed strained business and personal relations between elements of both communities; the most common outlet being to switch off the television or radio news when visitors were present. That way at least, some painful discussions were avoided, and not least with the Irish community itself, for whom the Ulster escalation proved divisive. A million people, albeit Irish, cannot live by-and-large contentedly in Britain without feeling some degree of loyalty for the ways and mores of that country. Thus the Irish Guards regiment of the British Army, for instance, have since the 1900s drawn heavily from among the Irish in Britain—and it would be a foolhardy accuser who would speculate on their loyalty to Queen and Country.

All through the Ulster troubles, Irishmen served in the British Army in Northern Ireland. Some such indeed were killed or wounded. The overriding divisiveness, however, lay with the ingrained attitude of the Irish community, which found itself in the nebulous position of desiring the withdrawal of a British military presence in Ireland while at the same time being grateful to benefit from the variegated offerings of life in Britain. Put another way, the Irish in Britain are happy to avail themselves of the advanced social welfare system which—to extend the logic of nationalistic political sympathies—they would deny their compatriots in Northern Ireland. When it comes to extreme political agitation, it is a contradiction which most are not unaware of.

The fact that such a small proportion actively engage in agitation about the Ulster situation is another telling commentary on the extent to which the Irish, as a community, have become absorbed into the British spectrum in recent years. They are loathe to put at risk their prime concern of day-to-day living; indeed for the majority the word 'politician' does not evoke any meaningful response. As Eamonn McCann, left-wing revolutionary and friend of Bernadette Devlin, says: 'There is no horde of proletarian Irish ... ready and waiting to pour out from Camden Town, Cricklewood and Kilburn to stop the heart of Empire. They are too worried about the rent rises announced last month by the Greater London Council.'

And that, really, is the nub of the matter and death-knell of appreciable political radicalism among the immigrants. What have the million or so Irish in Britain to be radical about, when all their civil, religious, and social rights are given to them? and in a 'foreign' country: more rights indeed than most of them could hope for in 'Ould Ireland' of Saturday night chanting nostalgia. For the majority of that million Irish in Britain have bitter-black memories of their materially inopportune youth in Ireland and of the failure of the Republic to provide them with the glories so fiercely promised by the visionary creators of that state in 1916. As one weary agitator remarked: 'All they're good for now is cursing the English on Saturday night with their free National Health teeth.'

'... National Health teeth' is relevant. The unlikely spectacle of a million Irish in Britain demanding with one voice the immediate withdrawal of Britain from Northern Ireland would be a supreme irony—given that that community eagerly and gratefully accept the benefits of the British Welfare structure here. (As a pertinent aside, the Irish in Britain in 1970 had access to social services costing £170 per head of population, whereas the comparative figure for the Irish Republic was £68 per person.)

The writer Claud Cockburn put it another way, in his column in the *Irish Times*. They were, he said, 'more interested in proving themselves a cut above the Pakistani'. And that too has relevance, for most remember the 'No Irish' signs of the forties and fifties. The pressures of history dictate that they be cautious and conservative. Any guilt-feelings they may have about 'Ould Ireland' can be quickly allayed by a trip home and the dramatic contrast between the range of opportunities available to them in their own homeland compared with those available in Britain. The economic base underlying post-famine immigration is an all-powerful one. The mass of the Irish in Britain are content with their lives here: many indeed find their situation to be one of rewarding challenge and achievement. Only a tiny proportion of those settled—around five thousand—return in any one year. The remainder have neither time nor temperament for headline heroics, but have instead the private heroism of having pulled themselves up by their bootstraps. They of 'the middle nation' embody the tenet that the first responsibility of the Irish in Britain is to the Irish in Britain. They are, by and large, on good terms with their neighbours and reasonably well adjusted to their adopted environment. Their children will grow up to become the 'Brit-Irish' with mixed feelings. They have no desire to fly a tricolour over Camden Town, and though they pay ritual lip-service to flying one over Belfast they will not do much to aid that fluttering. When it comes to political radicalism, the Irish in Britain react with the unspoken awareness of a more personal corollary: that of their own communal struggle in overcoming the material disadvantages of being born in Ireland and the patently lesser disadvantages of living now in Britain. That they may go unhindered about that effort is to them sufficient 'radicalism' to the day.

In Business

If the sixties were notable for the improvement of the immigrants' living standards, and their developing and participating in the political mainstream, it was also the decade which saw their increasing involvement in business. As their involvement with the Labour Party sprang essentially from grass-roots identification with the personality of that party, so did their emergence in business reflect their own grass-roots activity in two industries, building and drink.

They had, since the Great Famine exodus of the mid-nineteenth century, been prominent in construction trades as navvies and workmen. By the turn of the century the tradition had become so well established that the hardy men of the Irish western seaboard—and most other rural areas—had little thought for any other kind of work upon arrival in Britain. Indeed their Irish adolescence was filled with tales and jargon of English building sites, of 'shuttering' and 'four by two's', of jigs and joists and cranes and all the technical paraphernalia of the building site. Every Irish schoolboy knows the popular parody of answer to the Penny Catechism question which asks:

> Who made the World?
> McAlpine,[1] sir!

Most Irish adolescents know too, of the legendary 'big money' to be made in the building sites. Inevitably, the Irish who spent most of their working lives digging down and building up in Britain bequeathed some expertise to their children, so that by the 1930s many small construction firms were owned by first-generation Irish. The occasional family effort blossomed into larger-scale enterprise, such as Gleeson's, but by and large most firms of Irish origin remained medium-sized until the building boom which followed the Second World War. It was this post-

[1] A well-known British construction firm.

war expansion which opened the hard-graft path to development and riches. Vast reaches of cities needed to be rebuilt, new towns and housing estates were on the drawing-boards of every major local authority in the country. The one group ready and eager to rebuild Britain were the Irish. In the London-Irish dance halls of the Blitz a cheer would sometimes break out upon the fall of a nearby bomb, not for any reason of racial animosity, but rather for the prospect of building work on the morrow. One man who has a vivid recollection of that period (and who prefers to remain anonymous) came to the Midlands as a raw adolescent from the west of Ireland. He took up trade as a plasterer, slept two to a bed in homely digs: 'If you weren't up by an early hour, the landlady got you up. I've seen grown men having their bare arses slapped.' He scrupulously attended his religious duties, hunted among compatriots for a copy of 'The Western' (*Western People*, his home-town newspaper) and hit for London and acres of plastering in the post-war building boom.

In London he settled in digs near Camden Town, was offered more work than he could cope with and took on a friend. Even then he could not plaster all he was offered so he contracted-out to another. Today, twenty-five years later, he presides over a multiplicity of construction interests, with an annual turnover of millions, and has belatedly time to indulge in the cultural interests which he denied himself in the helter-skelter of fortune building. His story has been repeated, to a varying degree, among many others of the Irish builders who came to 'dig for gold in the streets'. Their prime attribute was hard work, allied to that ambition common to émigrés the world over, namely the desire to have some achievement or material wealth as reward for the very act of exile. With the predominance of the Irish in the building industry, the very fact of being Irish was, of course, in itself an advantage, a factor which applied particularly to the rural Irish, who are more dour, insular, and unco-operative with outsiders.

The Irish have become so influential in the building industry that on certain big money jobs it's not sufficient merely to be Irish to get work. In certain areas, one must come from a particular county in Ireland! Sections of the Victoria Line—London's latest underground artery which travels under the Thames—were built by teams of Donegal men who jealously guarded the big earnings for themselves. (One of their games, when bored, was to find who could toss a bag of cement farthest.)

Certainly for the entrepreneurial-minded Irishman, the ability to handle and lead his own countrymen was a necessary ingredient of the rise to forming his own company. Often he was helped by his brothers, for in that hierarchy of family maleness lay, in effect, the sort of sophisticated management structure that I.B.M. and I.C.I. try so expensively to maintain. At its most basic, the advantage of a group of brothers forming a company was that it would take a very brave man indeed to 'cross' them on a deal: in the early days of a new company's life the reputation of a group of brothers stood them in good stead when a challenge—often physical—arose from some quarter or other.

Hardly surprising, then, to note that the six leading Irish construction companies in Britain are all commanded by brothers; brothers who in most cases have come up through the ranks together, having started their working lives by digging down and staying on to build up business empires. The flair, panache, and toughness of these brotherly enterprises have given rise to many legends within the Irish community, such as the Irish contractor whose tender to construct the 'Chunnel'—the projected tunnel under the English Channel to France—was so low in price that he was called in by the Government officers to elaborate. The contractor explained the low tender on the grounds that his business was a family one: his brother would start tunnelling from Dover while he himself would start at Calais, and they would meet in the middle of the Channel. 'But supposing you don't meet?' he was asked. 'Ah, well then, we'll give ye two tunnels for the price of one.'

Similar stories contribute to the mystique of how fortunes were made and construction groups fashioned by lowly labourers from rural Ireland. Of how a large plant-hire firm owes its origins to the morning when two brothers took leave of a building site—in the company of a hoist. And of how that hoist and a few picks and drills which had been 'collected' from the building site were later seen in a yard over which hung the proud family inscription of the brothers' names as plant-hire providers. And of how, ten years later, the two enterprising brothers now preside over a group whose annual plant investment runs at half a million.

These are the stories that Irish labourers like to tell as they quench the drought of a hard day's graft. The implication being that perhaps one of these days they themselves will take the first plunge into sub-contracting, after which there will be no looking back, but only forward to Jaguar cars and drawing-board chat and the big house in London's Highgate (up the hill from Camden Town).

Underneath such romanticism, however, lies the hard graft of effort. None of the Irish construction firms were built up on an eight-hour day, but rather on long hours, every day of the week. And to the detriment, in personality terms, of many of the founders of these companies. The narrow concentration upon the mechanics of building, the long hours, the incessant travel, and the near-total immersion of energy in the business has left many of these men materially wealthy but culturally impoverished. Some, wisely, perceive the signs of personality disintegration and hand over control to a son, or to colleagues. Others cling on, in spite of all medical or family advice to the contrary, for their companies are their lives' work and often the only real 'thing' in their lives, the prop-up of vanity and of their very personalities. For them, work takes the lion's share of their energies, leaving them as powerful builders of motorways and housing estates and, by the same token, painfully inadequate in many other areas of social and cultural activity.

Take, as example, the progression of a young man from insular rural Ireland, who left school at thirteen, takes the emigrant boat at fifteen, becomes a ganger on a London building site at twenty-one, a partner in a small sub-contracting firm at twenty-five, and a wealthy man in his forties; who by sheer dint of experience and toughness finishes housing estates within penalty-clause schedule. That man may never have the motivation to read one book (except a thriller) or realize his potential in other areas of his personality. The desire to 'get on', the later success in doing so, and the subsequent demands of consolidating that success leave many such successful builders bereft of fulfilment in the 'cultural' areas of their personality.

This is not to take a churlish view of their otherwise impressive achievements, but rather to recognize the penalties exacted by the rigours of their life's effort. Certainly the men who came to prominence in the sixties are more aware of the world about them than their predecessors: one heartening change, for instance, has been the extent to which some successful Irish businessmen have recently involved themselves in the welfare of their less well-off compatriots. Increasingly in recent years have a handful of businessmen contributed to the expansion of social welfare services among the Irish community, to helping with time, talent, and money towards the expansion of Irish centres throughout Britain. At a more individual level there is one dramatic example known to this writer of a man who founded and master-minded a construction firm to the expansion of a multi-million corporation, who in his forties went to university and gained a business degree with speed. Partially, no doubt, to be conversant with the management language of his college-trained executives, but also to prove happily he could do it.

The company he had helped build in Britain—Abbey Homesteads—was left in the care of his younger brother, Charles Gallagher. Under the latter's entrepreneurial guidance the company by 1971 had an annual turnover of £5,000,000, its seven hundred employees had accounted for 20,000 new homes and it had built housing estates in Cyprus. Charles Gallagher himself is a powerful and benevolent figure among the Irish community in London and currently superintending the expansion of the Irish Centre in Camden Town.

At a similar level of business and community impact is Tony Beatty, an accountant by profession and a tycoon by instinct. With a background of the typical immigrant coming from rural Ireland, Beatty slogged nights to gain his accountancy qualifications, built up clients among the Irish immigrant building community, founded his own consultancy, and is now the wealthy director of many concerns including a merchant bank. Much of his initial business activity was among the Irish; financial, taxation, and accountancy advice to small and medium-sized builders. Latterly he has expanded his business interests to include catering, car-hire, travel, and holidays. His investments and clients are now about equally divided between Irish and British. The significance of entrepreneurs such as Charles Gallagher, Tony Beatty, and others is that, having made their pile, so to speak, they remain involved in the welfare at large of the émigré community which has, in a sense, produced them. Not the least contributory influence upon the upgrading of that community during the sixties has been the effective interest of part of the Irish business community in providing material help and advice.

The dual business success of the Irish in building and public house management—and its reference to the community—may be best seen in the expansion of the Irish Centres in the major towns and cities. These centres provide a much needed meeting and recreation ground for the mainly rural immigrants and have attached to them trained social workers who perform a multitude of tasks to ease the culture shock of the more inadequate in transferring from a warm social life in Ireland to the more impersonal hurly-burly existence in a British city.

The expansion of these centres in the sixties was considerably aided by Irish builders who fulfilled the building requirements at a marginal profit (or at cost) and by British brewing companies who advanced the necessary funds in return for the monopoly contract as drink suppliers to the centres. That the breweries should thus so confidently loan substantial amounts of money to one ethnic group is explained by their confidence in that ethnic group as consumers and purveyors of their products. It comes as no surprise, somehow, to learn that half the eight thousand public houses in the London area are managed or controlled by Irishmen. Like the construction industry, their success in this field is due to a combination of tradition, flair, and essentially hard work.

There is also the critical factor of being master in their own house which appeals so strongly to the Irish as a race. It is the ambition of most young Irish barmen to gain control of their own premises, which most duly do, having served time with two 'guv'nors' and been recommended by them to a brewery for tenancy.

All businesses have their 'dishonesties'. The construction and drink trade are no exception. Underpinning the émigré success in both are two sensitive areas, needful of comment. In the building trade it is the practice known as 'lumping': in the pub business, the fiddle is known as 'buying outside'.

'The lump' refers to sub-contracted labour which is paid by the hour or day and is neither insured, registered, nor officially recorded. This, briefly, is how it operates. Take the case of a large contract, where a variety of jobs will be sub-contracted by the main contractor: site excavation, clearance, foundations, services, walls, floors, ceilings, etc. These will be sub-contracted to smaller firms who will employ additional labour. This additional casual labour will be paid at a daily rate, the rate varying according to the skill. Where 'the lump' operates, the daily rate is paid without the deduction of income tax or insurance. The sub-contractor has gained the contract on a fixed sum. Where he can make excess profits is in the difference between the amount *claimed* for labour and what he *actually pays his labour*. I understand the addition of fictitious names was, until recently, commonplace. A sub-contractor would include in his tender, say, thirty men at £8 per day for twenty days to complete the specified work. In reality he would employ, say, twenty-five men thereby ensuring himself an immediate excess profit. It was almost impossible to challenge his figures, as no precise records of names and insurance details were kept.

Undoubtedly many contractors and sub-contractors grew rapidly rich on 'the lump'. Undoubtedly, too, the system was not confined to the Irish, though temperamentally it suited them well, offering the advantages of tax-free earnings and freedom from irksome officialdom. The system appealed, too, to the Irish labourer's desire to be a free agent and to work and travel at will. 'The lump' provided him with good money for hard work and no bother from the English tax man! It solidified his sense of being in Britain for a short time and nurtured the illusion of 'going home next year'. The disadvantages were, of course, that most often he did not 'go home next year' but stayed on for most of his adult life. The penalties of such fond illusion, and of 'the lump', were brought sharply home if he fell ill or was injured. Then, for all his years' hard labour and easy money, there were no welfare benefits. I recall the middle-aged Irishman with whom I regularly played darts in a North London pub. One evening blood seeped from his leg to the pub-floor. I helped him to the toilet where he dripped blood into the bowl from a broken vein, and tied a tourniquet. He refused to be helped to a near-by hospital, on the grounds that 'they would only want me name and address'. He had lived fifteen years in Britain, worked mainly on the building sites under 'the lump' and was terrified of bureaucracy. Probably a proportion of those high earnings had been faithfully remitted to a family in Ireland, but now in his middle-age he had little to show for the years except a single room, his game of darts, and fear of the authorities. He was a simple, civilized man. There are thousands like him among the Irish in Britain upon whose bent and labouring backs many an Irish fortune has been built.

For better or worse, that system is rapidly declining: April 1972 sounded the death-knell of 'the lump', officially at least. From that date all building labour was required to be scrupulously registered, and though some Irish contractors will mourn the demise of 'the lump', the majority will adjust to the change for they have, in the sixties, become more adjusted to the permanence of their stay in Britain.

Those grown rich upon the system are now mostly 'respectable' and eager to be accepted as such. For whatever its demerits, 'the lump' did allow the immigrant Irish to gain a foothold and consolidate their claim upon an environment which, literally, they helped to build. Criticisms of the Irish labour force in the construction industry most often centre about their capacity to skimp bureaucracy—they work under false names and pay no Income Tax—but the criticisms ignore the fact that such omissions are not confined to the Irish. Indeed such practices grew up with the industry—as did the

Irish—but the habits of evasion were rife long before the Irish became prominent.

Perhaps the best example of the decline of 'the lump' are the hundreds of thousands of building workers who, this year, will be registered under the tax category of 'Schedule D', for the self-employed. Hand-in-hand with the current decline in 'the lump' is the increase in Irish-owned construction firms and interests, and more significantly, the growing number of Irish executives in the large British building corporations such as Wimpey and Laing. They have, in a sense, come over 'the lump', of early labouring, of being 'hewers of wood and drawers of water', and progressed to being an integrated and potent force in the construction industry.

OF PUBS AND PUBLICANS

In the area of drink and public houses, their rise has been, if anything, more dramatic and again most clearly seen in the sixties. It was predictable, perhaps, that they should make such an impact upon that area of leisure, given the traditional sacred place of the pub in native Irish society. In the rural towns and villages from which most immigrants came, the pub is the natural business and social centre, the latter-day equivalent of the Roman Forum, wherein the day-to-day business of the community is transacted. On par with the priest, the publican is the most influential figure, and the respository of as many secrets. (During two lengthy strikes by banking-staff in Ireland during the sixties, the pubs assumed the function of cashing cheques and advancing capital. Local publicans held as shrewd and informed knowledge of a client's credit-worthiness as did a bank manager.)

The demerit was, and is, the stagnant decay of the rural reaches, where little prospect of succession to such tribal power is offered to the rising generations. The young men who take the emigrant boat to England, thus conditioned by the pub-autocracy of their background, soon find a natural vocational outlet in dispensing alcohol to the cosmopolitan clientele of British cities. Often, of course, they find their first serving stint in an Irish house where the bulk of the custom is Irish.

The novice's capacity for handling the vagaries of his own people in the often tumultuous atmosphere of Irish pubs in Britain provides an early teething in pub (and people) management. The good order of many an 'Irish' public house is maintained not only by the understandable ability of the landlord to speak the language of his clientele, but also on occasion by his physical courage in quietening a punch-up. Consequently, the encouragement to Irish personnel by the various large and powerful British breweries is not due to any ethnic benevolence, but rather to the experienced assessment that the Irish, on the whole, make pretty competent tenants and managers. They work long and arduously, as demanded by the nature of the business, but having additionally the motive, common to many immigrant groups, of wishing to succeed. Thus most take an inordinate pride in the running of their houses and in imparting the classical bonhomie of the host. Many, also, make the much sought fortune, through a combination of hard work and good sense, flair, and 'buying outside'.

BUYING OUTSIDE

The majority of the 72,000 public houses in Britain are owned by breweries and are known as 'tied houses', i.e. the beer sold comes from the brewery owner. Most pubs are run by tenants or managers; the manager is on a fixed salary with a possible share of the profits, while the tenant, by contrast, formally buys his beer, wines, and spirits from the brewery and all the profits ensuing from subsequent sales are his. The tenant personally bears the cost of upkeeping and furnishing the premises, the salaries of staff and improvement; all, of course, geared to increased consumption and profits. Thus a tenant who combines flair with application may substantially increase his turnover of alcohol to a level which provides him, personally, with a substantial income. (A personal income of around £5,000 a year is not uncommon from a house of busy trade.)

Where extra profit may be accrued is through the practice of 'buying outside', by which the tenant, having increased beer sales to a level satisfactory to the owning brewery, then purchases additional stock from another supplier at rates more profitable to himself.

Hardly surprising, then, that most émigré Irish prefer the tenancy of a house, and will often bid large sums—from £3,000 upwards—to secure the tenancy of a 'good' house. Family feeling operates considerably here, in that a successful elder brother will often recommend his younger brother for a tenancy, and provide the necessary initial finance to get him started. Often, too, the bulk of local trade will be Irish, extending to social and sporting clubs using the premises regularly for meetings and business. There is also the interaction of construction, public house, and community interests: an Irishman, having accrued capital through a building interest, will often invest that capital in purchasing a pub tenancy and at some later date help set up a former workmate as publican. Equally his premises will be available for a benefit dance to raise funds for the family of a former workmate killed or injured on a building site.

As the practice of 'lumping' grew up with the construction industry, so did the system of 'buying outside' develop with the licensed trade. In recent years, however, the benign tolerance of the breweries to such practice has somewhat diminished. At least one of the major brewers now increasingly prefers to install managers rather than tenants.

As the sixties witnessed the developing influence of the Irish at management levels of the construction industry, so were the Irish-run public houses improving their décor and facilities and the general quality of their premises, without, for the most part, turning their backs on the bulk of hard-drinking trade. Thus in many Irish-run public houses the labourers from a near-by building-site feel free to inhabit the carpeted lounge after work, knowing themselves to be a valued part of an ethnic trade. Similarly Saturday night in the areas of, say, Camden or Kentish Town in London, or Sparkbrook in Birmingham is awash with alcoholic nostalgia for things Irish. And though the décor and carpeting may be new, the plaintive songs are nineteenth-century indulgences, badly crooned, in the main, against an atmosphere of cigarette smog and sullen faces. (Whatever the other diverse effects of emigration from Ireland, the 'typically Irish' pub of a Saturday night is, to this writer at least, depressing. Gathered into smoky congress, subject to an unceasing din of spurious nostalgia, the former inhabitants of rural towns and villages in Ireland summon to mind the ghettoism of the 'coffin-ships' of enforced migration. The stray English visitor on a Saturday night in North London may wonder if he is still in England as he vainly searches for a quiet 'English' pub in the outer reaches of Islington or Hammersmith.)

If the Irish in London are thus prominent in the pub trade, they are less so in the provinces. In the southern counties they are to be found in farming, market-gardening, and racehorse training. (One of the Queen Mother's two horse trainers is an Irishman.) In the west Midlands they are prominent as managers of supermarkets. In the Midlands, a chain of dry-cleaning shops is Irish-owned; at white collar level generally there is a sprinkling in banking and insurance. But in the mainstream of big business, there is but tiny Irish representation. In the Stock Exchange and in the upper managerial echelons of finance groups and large corporations Irish representation is minute, certainly by contrast with, say, Jewish representation. It could, of course, be argued that democratic British representation in these areas is equally low; the Stock Exchange for instance, being mainly a warren of family and public school connections. The obvious cause of lack of Irish impact in these areas is one of tradition—the Ireland which produced the mass of the Irish in Britain was under-industrialized and consequently unable to provide the training and skills required in these areas. (The sixties brought some improvement: the Gross National Product in Ireland in that decade rose by 125 per cent and the average annual industrial growth was 7 per cent.)

The decade also saw the establishment of 500 new industrial projects with attendant training (often abroad) in new industrial skills for a generation of Irish in Ireland. This new industrialization was perceptible among the recent immigrants to Britain, most dramatically in the new breed of Irish executives, of whom Tony O'Reilly is a prime example. O'Reilly, a former Rugby International, moved from Ireland to Britain in

1969, but hardly as a traditional immigrant. He came rather as Managing Director of Heinz, U.K., the British section of the multi-million foods corporation. And when he arrived in a chauffeur-driven limousine to turn out for the local London-Irish rugger team at suburban matches, the image of the traditional Irish immigrant took a severe knocking.

O'Reilly is a product of the industrial boom of the early sixties in Ireland, and the consequent adaption to new managerial skills—with relevant effects upon immigrants to Britain. The growth of an Irish employment agency in London, Emerald Staff Agency, mirrors this improvement. When the agency began in 1959, it specialized in placing Irish workers in the catering and hotel trade. Ten years later, it had sprouted branch offices in predictable parts of London—Hammersmith, Shepherds Bush, Clapham—and broadened the variety of skills on offer to British firms, in response to the more skilled quality of immigrants from Ireland. A measure of this improved quality was demonstrated in 1970 when the Emerald Agency supplied over a hundred computer personnel direct from Ireland to help staff a giant computer complex of the National Westminster Bank in London. Ten years earlier that numerical strength of skills would simply have been non-existent in Ireland; a time when factory managers on a Croydon industrial estate complained that Irish workers were incompetent and fumbling in dealing with precision assembly work.

An equally significant pointer to this changing reality was the entry of a leading Irish banking combine into the British market, depending initially on the increased affluence of the immigrants. Allied Irish Banks in 1970 established a full banking service to the general public in the dominantly-Irish district of Kilburn in London; almost every Irishman of financial substance in the half-million strong London-Irish community was present at the dinner to celebrate the bank's opening venture into the British market. The bank's hospitality and pre-launch intelligence operation was amply rewarded in subsequent months when it gathered in £1,000,000 worth of accounts, most of which came from the Irish community, and were mainly business accounts. A third of the customers were non-Irish. One year after opening, the branch held accounts totalling £2,000,000 and received an accolade normally reserved for branches of the Big Five (British) banks, that of being raided by gangsters. Allied Irish now have ten banking branches in Britain, almost all centred upon areas of strong Irish communities, but with the clientele being about one third non-Irish and the projection indicating a levelling-off at around half-and-half Irish-British clients. From the point of view of business expansion, the slogan may well be: 'First find your ethnic market.' With a million Irish-born in Britain, this is a philosophy being further investigated by Irish-based manufacturers eager to gain a foothold on the wider U.K. market. The sixties saw this ethnic market being tapped by Irish manufacturers of cigarettes, confectionery, and foodstuffs.

A brief look at the history of the consumer-drink, Guinness, provides a pointer to the possibilities of the ethnic market. First brewed in Dublin in 1759, the drink was supplied from there to a growing British market for almost two hundred years. Being in the nature of a national drink in Ireland, its increased consumption in Britain initially rested on the loyalty of Irish immigrants who helped make it popular among the working-classes generally: it was not until 1936 that its consumption in Britain required the establishment of a brewery here. Today, when Guinness is a name in the 130 countries of foreign export, the company preserves its contact with the Irish. In Dublin the company is the largest private employer of labour and in terms of staff relations and welfare schemes sets a lead for every other Irish concern. It also donates substantial annual amounts to charities. Among the Irish in Britain, the company keeps equally strong and benevolent links, generously supports socio-cultural events in the community and has, for instance, underwritten the substantial overdraft of the Irish Club in London's Eaton Square.

In recent years, Irish-based companies have made substantial inroads into the British market. Swan-Ryan International, a company controlled by entrepreneur Dermot Ryan, now holds half the U.K. packaged holiday business. Half the annual premium income of an Irish insurance company emanates from Britain. In August 1973, the Smurfit Group of Dublin paid £10,000,000 for the print and packaging concerns of a U.K. company. While in the traditional fields of agricultural produce, the export agencies for Irish milk, beef, and butter have expanded their share of the British market.

In the reverse direction, the talents of successful business-men from among the Irish in Britain have been channelled back to Ireland, through the London-based lobbying of the Industrial Development Authority (a body sponsored by the Irish Government) which informs entrepreneurs of industrial development opportunities in Ireland and provides substantial grants towards the initiation of new industries, particularly in the areas most depleted through emigration.

Each successive year of the sixties has witnessed an increase in such return investment of finance and skills—a measure of the growth of the Irish business community in Britain. There is also evidence of a substantially increased return of finance to Irish banking institutions, principally investment and de-posit account renderings which qualify for tax-free interest. It may be remarked, however, that the newly-acquired afflu-ence of the community during the last decade has not been proportionately matched by contributions from the business sector towards the welfare of the community generally: the 'community sense' of individuals noted earlier being character-istic of but a minority of the business sector. This lack of community cohesion is most noticeable in the area of social problems such as adolescent delinquency, alcoholism, and general inadequacy where the major activity of prevention and rehabilitation rests substantially with the combined efforts of British statutory agencies and Catholic Church interests—the contribution from the business community being extremely meagre. This paucity of effort from the newly affluent occa-sioned one priest, prominent in the London-Irish community, to remark that affluence was 'producing a breed of vulgar, materialistic savages. God help Ireland when she becomes prosperous, if this is how we behave when we get some money.' Another observer remarked that 'we're breeding a race of Irish Jews over here', with unconscious contradiction, for the self-help of British Jewry startlingly highlights the absence of similar organized welfare among the Irish. It may well be, of course, that the various racial persecutions of the Jews has left them with a more concerted awareness of the need for self-help than the Irish, though a visit to any Irish club with its relentless décor of green shamrocks would appear to belie that easy explanation. The more likely explanation for lack of Irish welfare cohension may reside in a combination of factors; the fact that growth of the business sector, while being substantial, is comparatively recent; and the fact that for many there is an indecision of identity, an ambivalence as to fully accepting Britain as 'home'.

Nevertheless, some of the changes of the past decade indicate that this 'crisis of identity' is being resolved, at least in the attitude of some pioneering individuals towards efforts of community self-help.

But the weighty spectrum of the professional and business community, by contrast to such isolated endeavours, is characterized by a distinct absence of community awareness—while containing in its recent growth the potential to considerably aid the well-being not only of the Irish in Britain, but in Ireland. The annual remittance to relatives in Ireland of over £10,000,000 from among the 'ordinary' Irish immigrants is but an indication of the resources available in the professional-business sector of the community.

Whether this potential can be effectively harnessed is a matter of radical influence upon the entire pattern of Irish immigration, and on those who inhabit that twilight area of what is politely called 'social problems'.

With some 'Social Problems'

Between 1950 and 1960, the contribution of the Irish to violent crime in London rose from 9.7 per cent to 12.2 per cent —yet they formed only 2 to 3 per cent of the population of the metropolis.[1]

In the same decade, Irish-born from the Republic accounted for 12 per cent of the prison population of England, Scotland, and Wales—yet only 2 per cent of the total population were Irish-born.

In 1966, a study undertaken in Birmingham demonstrated that the Irish were responsible for: 23 per cent of violent crime; 20 per cent of property offences; 17 per cent of offences of prostitution; 60 per cent of offences for drunkenness. Yet Irish-born formed but 7 per cent of the population of the area studied.[2]

These excerpts summarize what to many native British is the 'Irish Question', i.e. the presence of an immigrant community with a capacity for drunkenness, fighting, and court appearances. Much of the Irish over-representation in the various criminal studies of the past ten years is indeed due to a combination of drunkenness and domestic dispute, allied to the propensity to 'let fly' at a protagonist. Fist-fighting is a strong cultural strain in the Irish, not generally regarded as offensive, even in middle-class ethos; by and large tolerated and, on occasions, admired. (By no means all Irish fights are as sporting as the Irish themselves would like to believe. I have seen many vicious fights in Irish pubs, with bottles and boots liberally used. The knife, however, is usually alien to an all-Irish fight.)

But given the propensity for 'clouting' and for inebriation, the Irish in Britain appear disproportionately prominent in crime statistics. Being dismissive of that oft-quoted comment

[1] F. H. McLintock, *Crimes of Violence*, London: Macmillan, 1963.
[2] John Lambert, *Crime, Police and Race Relations*, a study in Birmingham, Oxford University Press, 1970.

on statistics—'there are three kinds of lies: lies, damned lies, and statistics'—and looking rather to the hidden variables pertaining to the above comparisons, one finds that the very composition of the Irish émigré grouping makes them prone to a high appearance in law-breaking statistics. (1) Most crime is committed by males between fifteen and forty-four, in which groups there are disproportionately high numbers of Irish, compared to the native population. (2) The Irish are over-represented among the urban poor, and among the inhabitants of decaying city areas where the crime rate, anyway, is high.

There is also the critical element of 'culture-shock', the effects upon the personality of moving from one community to another. As the author of the Birmingham report, John Lambert, says:

> Release from the stringent controls of the home society provokes something of a reaction which finds expression in relatively greater crime and disorder, theft, and drunkenness —the expression of those for whom immigration has not brought economic security, stable family relations, and other signs of success in this new country.

The culture-shock of transference undoubtedly accounts for a good deal of criminality, particularly at the level of petty thievery and drunkenness among adolescents who in Ireland would have less opportunity for such indulgence. At its simplest, parental influence is sufficient to inhibit such activities. The absence of family influence is perhaps the first culture-shock awareness of adolescent immigrants. At a deeper, and perhaps more meaningful level, the very act of transference from one contrasting environment to another can induce detrimental personality effects. At its most superficial, the departure from a close tribal society, heavily laden (and propped up) with myth and superstition induces a feeling of nakedness and vulnerability. The new environment initially presents problems, not least of language and manners. The expressions 'please' and 'thank you', for instance, are much more widely used in English society, at all levels, than in Ireland. And the fact that all Irish immigrants speak English is of little help: the assumption from the host society being that because the Irish speak English, then they should have English manners. Similarly, the myths of Irish history hang in the brain of many an Irishman, who expects the English to measure-up to the awe-inspiring imperial caricatures of his nationalistic Irish education, and is somewhat thrown to find instead a rather disinterested, polite, self-sufficient people. The English in turn may express some disillusion if the Irishman be found to be abstemious, or dull or unable to sing! (It may surprise English readers to know that Ireland, on the whole, contains a higher proportion of teetotal adults than Britain. Equally, readers in Ireland should know that many Englishmen care not a fig for the lost Empire and are, in fact, rather glad to be rid of it.) Relations between the races are thus inhibited and thrown lop-sided by the weight of mutually inherited myths, to the extent that, by and large, both races prefer the company of their own and can mix better with other nationalities, than with each other.

New immigrants, while being curious about the English, are also often highly sensitive to the real or imagined differences. A common mutual reaction among new immigrant Irish is that of interpreting the routine curtness of metropolitan shop assistants as a reaction to their own Irish accent, often keenly felt by women and adolescents accustomed to the more relaxed manners of Ireland. All this, of course, is taken in stride by the average well-adjusted immigrant and the passage of time, of necessity, blunts such prickly first impressions. But where these sensitivities can be critical is in the cases of immigrants already vulnerable through personality disorders. In this regard, the Irish authorities have little to be proud of, having condoned through successive generations the export of Ireland's mentally ill to Britain. The failures of the post-Revolutionary Irish Governments are legion, but in the context of this chapter, their neglect of the Irish émigrés is relevant.

In the past fifty years of independence, Irish Governments have paid only the minimum of attention to that other third of their population who resided semi-permanently in Britain. They did little to alleviate the travel conditions of the thirties, forties, and fifties when thousands of émigrés travelled to

Britain in overcrowded, insanitary conditions reminiscent of the coffin-ships of the previous century.

They offered little active encouragement towards the setting up of welfare centres, though one of the recommendations of a Government-sponsored commission[3] had been that the Government should urgently provide such aid. Indeed the general feeling at Government level in the forties and fifties was one of gratitude that Britain provided a safety-valve for the excess of unemployed, or as one of the commission's members, Mr Alex Fitzgerald, said: 'High emigration ... releases social tensions which would otherwise explode and makes possible a stability of manners and customs which would otherwise be subject to radical change.'

Mr Fitzgerald also declined to accept the view that 'a high rate of emigration is necessarily a sign of national decline. It is clear that in the history of the Catholic Church, the rôle of Irish emigrants has been significant. In the order of values, it seems more important to preserve and improve the quality of Irish life and therefore the purity of that message which our people have communicated to the world, than it is to reduce the numbers of Irish emigrants.' Those published remarks in 1953 were doubtless of immense consolation to the 33,000 emigrants who left Ireland that year and who were, for the most part, unwilling economic deportees. As they trudged off the mail-boats which daily berthed at Holyhead, their sense of abandonment must indeed have been lightened by the knowledge that their departure thus maintained 'the purity of that message which our people have communicated to the world'. They could, perhaps, have taken similar consolation from the views of one Irish historian of the period, who noted that 'had it not been for the safety-valve of emigration (400,000 in round figures for the decade 1950–60) the frustration of those years in Ireland would have led to mass riots'.

The immigrant boats, for the record, were depressing experiences—huddled anxious families, punctuated by the more ribald adolescents masking their uncertainty with hollow carousing. Then the bleary-eyed arrival into some strange city

[3] *Commission on Emigration and Other Population Problems, 1948–54*, Dublin: Stationery Office, 1954.

in the bleak hours and, for those without contacts, a trudge through strange streets in search of accommodation and eventually, work. Hardly surprising then that the inadequate and disturbed shortly found themselves in the care of one of the British welfare agencies.

What agencies in the peak-departure decade of the fifties attempted to help the inadequate? Not the Irish Government, as we have seen. Not the Irish middle-classes in Britain, fearful of their delicate (and imagined) status. The burden, in fact, lay with the British voluntary agencies who initiated sporadic measures, as did Irish Catholic lay organizations, such as the Legion of Mary and Knights of St Columba. In the event, the Catholic Hierarchy in Ireland made the first meaningful moves. Under pressure from priests in Britain the Irish Hierarchy established a scheme of emigrant chaplains who were assigned to areas of high Irish habitation. From the reports of these priests, telling of poor housing and high drinking and the isolation of the single labourer, came the decision to establish welfare centres with resident chaplains. The centres got under way in the late fifties and their subsequent accelerated growth is a comment not only (and obviously) on the need for such places, but on the range of difficulties faced by immigrants in integrating, even functionally, into native British society.

A measure of these difficulties is the figure of over 5,000 interviews/services rendered by the centres in 1970, a year in which 30,000 Irish entered Britain. In London, the centre at Camden Square provided help of one sort or another to 1,741 persons; the major efforts being in the areas of accommodation (1,337 services) and employment (997 services). The centre also helped thirty-three unmarried mothers and 105 cases of mental disturbance (schizophrenia, paranoia, acute depression). Five hundred of those assisted returned during the year for after-care help.

In the fifteen years since founding, the London centre has dealt with increased custom in each successive year. Together with the Liverpool and Birmingham centres, it has borne the brunt of welfare demands and is currently being expanded to double its size, with the emphasis on additional hostel accommodation and services. In 1970, the Catholic Hierarchy in

Ireland sponsored a 'once only' national collection for emigrants to Britain: of the £¼ million raised at church doors in Ireland, the bulk will be distributed among the centres in Britain to further what is, by any standard, a pioneering effort of ethnic self-help. Every area of major urban habitation now holds an Irish Centre, most of which are staffed with social workers. These centres are distinct from Irish clubs or dance-halls which have long been rooted in émigré areas and which mainly serve as drinking and dancing premises. The centres, by contrast, are engaged in energy and resource-stretching welfare work. Although they present a surfeit of things Irish, concerts, dancing-classes, bacon-and-cabbage dinners, underneath lies a concerned commitment to the upgrading of the emigrant's lot at the critical levels of housing, employment, and general welfare.

Regionally, the brunt of such work is borne by the centres in London, Liverpool, Manchester, and Birmingham. Smaller conurbations tend naturally to have a smaller number of problem cases and in many cases the Irish immigrants in provincial towns seem, even proportionately, to present fewer problems. One reason is that chronic housing shortage and urban stress upon the personality are metropolitan phenomena. The other reason may be that the majority of rural-originating émigrés find themselves more at home in a provincial town than in a large city. In Bristol, Gloucester, and Portsmouth, for instance, the Irish appear to blend more easily into the native fabric, to be more accepted as individuals and to form more valid relationships with the native population.

Cultural differences between England, Scotland, and Wales may be perceived in reaction to Irish immigration. Scotland is almost akin to Ulster in the separation of the communities in entrenched areas of Edinburgh and Glasgow: in that latter city, in the remnants of the Motherwell and Gorbals ghettos, the inherited siege-mentality persists. Football encounters between Rangers and Celtic teams are occasions for ritualistic displays of tribal extremism with Rangers being urged on to prove Scots-Protestant supremacy over the Celtic Irish-Catholic representation. All local police leave is cancelled for the year's series of matches and on the day following such encounters local magistrates are faced with an inevitable list of defendants. Rangers field non-Catholic players; Celtic mainly Catholic ones; Celtic fly the Irish tricolour, and travel abroad on Aer Lingus planes. The ghostly figures of the Protestant King William of Orange and the Catholic King James stalk the consciousness of the working districts of Glasgow, demanding due tribal loyalty from each successive generation of immigrants, a loyalty which, if emotively rendered, encourages the donor to risk appearing as a statistic in the city's annual crime figures. Given the sectarian traditions of Glasgow, it is hardly surprising to note that a higher proportion of Protestant-Irish emigrants from Ulster arrive there annually than to any other single conurbation in Britain.

In the rural areas of Scotland, Irish immigration follows the pattern laid down in the previous century's tradition of seasonal harvesting, potato-picking, and farm labouring, a tradition encased in the emigrant culture of the counties of Mayo and Donegal on the north-western Irish seaboard. Until the 1950s, whole families from these counties seasonally migrated to gather in the harvest in Ayrshire, Stirlingshire, Fife, and the Lothians, where each large farm had its 'bothie', a sort of open shed, which housed the migrant harvesters. They were paid according to their rate of clearance, at so much an acre harvested, and though they slept on straw beds and other facilities were primitive, in warm weather the system generally worked well.

By the fifties, however, a sinister element evolved. Whereas formerly local farmers contracted their own particular group of harvesters from Ireland, and generally treated them well, by the late fifties, a sort of Irish 'middle-man' had developed, intent on procuring maximum profit by offering their own working gangs to farmers. At this time the family migratory tradition had diminished, to be replaced with a flotsam of the inadequate and the delinquent. The outcome was the growth of an 'Irish Mafia' of contractors who brutalized their charges into excessive hours at low wages, and maintained, literally, a reign of terror over sections of the migrant labour. Workers who objected to the low wages were physically beaten, school-age youngsters were prevented from returning to Ireland, young girls were inveigled into promiscuity. It was, for the record, exploitation by the Irish upon the Irish.

Following newspaper revelations in the summer of 1971, the Scottish authorities attempted to alleviate the more blatant cases of hardship, but it is doubtful if the iniquities have been more than temporarily contained.

In Wales, few such sub-civilized ghettos exist. Indeed, of the three countries which make up Britain, Wales appears to offer the most relaxed and encouraging process of absorption. The 'continuum' of previous generations' descendants are representative of all levels of Welsh society and offer a hospitable texture of acceptance, extending in some instances to areas of employment which favour not only Welsh–Irish but present-day Irish immigrants. The work-force of a particular Cardiff factory, for instance, has since the 1900s been almost exclusively Irish, a protective reaction, perhaps, to the thunderings of Baptist preachers at the invading Catholic-Irish 'hordes' of the late nineteenth century. With growing urbanization the formerly strong religious identity of the Welsh has diminished somewhat and with it the strong antagonism towards the Irish has become diluted. And with the revival of Welsh self-assertion and nationalism, the immigrant Irish are becoming more accepted as allies rather than intruders.

In discussing the Irish émigrés as a 'social problem', due cognizance must be taken of the element of socio-cultural hostility which a minority still encounter in diverse areas. Anti-social behaviour in any immigrant group must to some degree be a response to native hostility. A possible pointer to the level of hostility, nationwide, was provided in a Gallup Survey of October 1967 which asked the question:

Do you think that on the whole this country has benefited or been harmed through immigrants coming to settle here from Ireland?

Answer:

Benefited 16 per cent; *Harmed* 22 per cent; *No difference* 46 per cent; *Don't know* 16 per cent.

In the cities of England, by and large, there is little overt antagonism and the work of the Irish centres can concentrate on those issues of housing and employment which are critical to anyone's sense of well-being, immigrant or no. In the welfare office of the Irish Centre in London's Camden Square, for instance, new immigrants and others requiring help are processed professionally: an extensive file of contacts is daily tapped for aid with employment and accommodation, the latter being absolutely necessary and in chronically short supply to the immigrant inflow into the burgeoning capital.

Such has been the overall contribution of such services—and of the chaplains and social workers—that the weight of Irish 'social problems' upon native British agencies has decreased in the last decade. By contrast, some of the techniques evolved from dealing with the problems of the Irish have been successfully applied to the wider British community at large.

The progress of one emigrant chaplain, Father Eamonn Casey, provides a dramatic example of such feedback. Casey, a tough-minded fluent priest from County Limerick, arrived as chaplain to the Irish community in Slough in 1960. His arrival coincided with the expansion of the town, with the growth of industry there and with the attendant increase in the numbers of Irish families and workers. In his view much of the disorientation, insecurity, and high alcoholic consumption he encountered among the Irish had one salient cause—shortage of decent, economically-priced housing. From that shortage, Father Casey felt, flowed most of the other symptoms of anti-social behaviour, particularly as the housing shortage most critically affected Irish families, most of whom, with families larger than the British average,[4] found it impossible to achieve home-ownership. Father Casey's solution was two-pronged. First, to raise a 'bank' of capital from the well-off, and secondly to raise the savings ability of those in need. He succeeded in both. Local industrialists and a sympathetic minority of local middle-classes were tapped for funds; with this initial 'bank' property was acquired and renovated and needful families installed at economic rents: for those who

---

[4] Special tabulations from the Census of 1961 *and* 1966 show that out of seven ethnic groups studied, the Irish have: the greatest number of children per family (2·52); the highest percentage of families with three or more children (42 per cent).

could afford more realistic rents, a proportion was held by Father Casey towards eventual house purchase on mortgage. A year after beginning there was sufficient inflow of capital in rents and savings and gifts to institute a system of financial gearing which maximized available (and growing) funds. From the priest's efforts and urging towards self-help grew a housing society which became expert in exploiting the hitherto disparate resources of local authority, family budgets, socialist-minded professional people, and building societies; to produce, within the capitalistic framework, a system socialist in attitude. The pioneering Slough effort made deep inroads upon the housing problems as well as other social problems, of the local Irish community. It also occurred at a time of nationwide housing problems; the blueprint has subsequently been adapted by other local authorities, particularly those with substantial immigrant communities, such as the London boroughs of Camden and Lambeth.

In other cities, the Catholic Housing Aid Society had been working along similar lines and in 1963 Father Casey became National Director of that body. Blooded, so to speak, by the Slough success, Casey now applied his expertise, and that of his lieutenants, to the wider national field. As National Director of the Society, Casey housed seven thousand people in the following five years of his directorship. Each successive year saw the Society move out from a Catholic-Irish base, into the wider community at large. Whereas in the early years the Irish accounted for 60 per cent of clients, the proportion of Irish has now levelled out at a third and the Catholic Housing Aid Society has become an influential agency of help to the community generally.

Thus in the past decade the social and settlement problems among the Irish have been tackled in the main by the Irish themselves. Most of the credit is due to the Irish Hierarchy, a body which rarely finds itself the object of praise from social scientists. (It could be argued that the traditional policies of the Catholic Church, in areas of education and family planning, are partially responsible for problems among emigrants.) Nevertheless, at a time when a potent minority among the Irish in Britain desperately needed help, when the British welfare agencies did their statutory best, the only other source from which intimate, professional help was forthcoming was from the Irish-Catholic Hierarchy.

Growing numbers of young priests were assigned to Britain in the fifties and sixties, many of them with new training in the social sciences. For a high proportion, the experience was salutary and disconcerting. They were, for the most part, products of Catholic families whose acceptance of the Church's teachings was total. Suddenly they encountered, among the emigrant Irish, attitudes which threatened their acceptance of unquestioned doctrine. More severely were the unconscious assumptions of Irish society thrown into sharp isolation; assumptions about the behaviour of adolescents, about the mobility of the men, and the chastity of the women. Working in the twilight areas of large cities, they encountered the Irishmen with common-law wives, Irishwomen engaged in prostitution, and adolescent drug-addicts. For a few the conflict between the mythology fondly fostered by the home society (all Irishmen are good, the women chaste, the adolescents innocent), and the reality of daily case-work was overwhelming and resulted in breakdown. During one year in the sixties, I understand, half a dozen of the fifty priests involved were repatriated because of ill-health. The point was taken by the Hierarchy. Now potential emigrant chaplains spend work periods in Britain during their training.

Certainly for the orthodox-minded priest, some of the personal ailments met with in a seething city could be bewildering. One priest in a North London parish assured me that what most of his callers needed was not a priest but a psychiatrist and he regarded his previous years in Africa as soft compared with the demands upon him in his London parish. His comments may be more relevant than he thought: many of his Irish callers were brought up in a society where the priest occupied a position which incorporated elements of the witch-doctor and the psychiatrist. But whether the traditional priestly training in Ireland is sufficient to cope with the complicated ills endemic in high-stress urban living is another matter.

To put it simply, the recitation of the Sixth Commandment

to a young unmarried mother is obviously of less use than some basic instruction in elementary techniques of family planning. But hardly any priests are equipped to render such advice (even if allowed to do so) and most lay social workers at Irish centres are loth to prescribe any advice at variance with Church teaching. Similarly, applicants with marital problems which are rooted in conflict over methods of contraception cannot be offered objective medical help.

Thus, in some elementary areas of Irish social work, the very system most involved is severely hampered by its own religious attitudes. Some chaplains and social workers privately admit this, and even criticize the narrow spectrum of Irish education generally. But until some further enlightenment affects the powers-that-be, there is little these workers in the field can do. At the time of writing there is little prospect of such advance, for almost all Irish education is controlled by the Church and though the creation of twenty-five Community Schools initially offered hope for a liberal-humanist education, that prospect too has dimmed. Speaking in Dublin in October 1971, the Primate of Ireland, Dr McQuaid, declared that the proposed Community Schools would be: 'Catholic in their management and teaching staff, in their discipline and curriculum ...' During the following month, opening a medical centre in the same city, the Archbishop implied that the centre—which trains one in three of the Republic's doctors in gynaecology—would not provide tuition in the general medical aspects of contraception. It wasn't until 1969 that Biology was introduced as a schools subject in Ireland, and then on a meagre level. Until recently there was no sex-education for the Republic's school-children (two out of five of whom on present trends will emigrate) which may account, in part, for the fact that Irish-born patients accounted for three-quarters of all European immigrants attending British clinics for the treatment of venereal diseases in 1962.[5]

Similarly, many factors which combine to produce inadequate emigrants can be traced to the Irish educational system, in particular to the dominating influence of the Church. It is,

[5] 'The Return of the Venereal Diseases', *British Medical Journal*, 23 June 1962.

of course, merely a truism to recite that many of the characteristics in any society which make for inadequate adults can be
traced to that society's socio-educational system, but it is a
truism which, on evidence, cannot be too often emphasized.

Certainly any concerned study of the problems among a
substantial minority of the Irish in Britain must inevitably lead
to a penetrating evalution of the educational structure in
Ireland. On present attitudes, any such radical evaluation is
unlikely to be countenanced, although confidential reports from
the emigrant chaplains must provide stimulus for hard-
thinking among the Catholic Hierarchy. One such report, currently with the Hierarchy, was compiled from an experimental
case-work study among Irish immigrant adolescents in London
during 1969–71.

The case-work was conducted at Benburb Base in the
borough of Camden—which gave generous help to the experi-
ment—and around five hundred Irish adolescents were offered
help in coming to terms with a wide variety of problems rang-
ing from the relatively simple matters of jobs and accommodation to the more taxing demands of personality disorders.
There were, too, cases of naïve prostitution among young girls,
and cases of petty criminality among male teenagers. The most
common symptom, in the social workers' judgements, was a
feeling of loneliness which they felt was traceable to early
family conflicts in Ireland, a loneliness which the victims
would ease with the transference across the Irish Sea, only to
find that the new pressures of urban living in a strange environment compounded these problems. Benburb Base, under
the care of a Belfast priest with training and experience in
social work (and therefore no stranger to such contemporary
urban-stress problems), has enjoyed some success in its experimental first year's effort. The report of its findings and
recommendations, currently before the Irish Hierarchy—and
the body's reaction—will determine the future character and
scope of the Base's efforts.

Thus in another critical area of immigrant vulnerability during the last decade have the Irish made inroads upon their
'social problems'. There are signs that the momentum of such
self-help will gather pace, from the combination of increased

awareness among the Irish community generally and the greater interest evinced among young social workers in Ireland. One area of distress, however, has been neglected—the area of drink and alcoholism.

ALCOHOL AND ALCOHOLISM

In 1966, when Irish-born formed 3 per cent of the population of London, a study of London's 'Skid Row' showed that the Irish formed 37 per cent of the sample studied. (Tabulated from the *Lancet*, 29 January 1966.) And the report of the Council for Social Welfare, 1970, was that Catholics in Britain have a higher proportion of alcoholics than any other religious denomination.

In the light of the above, it is almost facile to suggest that any discussion of alcoholism and the Irish should proceed from the acknowledgement that alcoholic drink permeates all levels of Irish life. Yet it is a necessary premise from which to proceed, for it explains the failure to contain the problem, and the reluctance to tackle a ruinous disease. The fact is that alcohol is enshrined in Irish life, and has been for centuries. In rhyme and rann, song and story, drink has become something of a sanctified Irish institution, by turns cursed and praised but never, in active consumption, ignored:

> Be you Cook's son, Earl's son or Duke's son
> Not one penny goes past the tombstone's brink
> So join the chorus, we've life before us
> When we put our one true trust in drink
> —from the Gaelic of 'Preab san Ol'
> (Trust in Drink) by Brendan Behan

It is tempting, as in so many other areas of Irish life, for Irishmen to simply blame the English for the national weakness for alcohol. History is rife with such comforting evidence and the case is easy to construct. One could begin with the fact that alcoholic drink is a reliever of stress and of untenable situations, and proceed to demonstrate that the vicissitudes of Anglo-Irish history reduced the Irish psyche to a state of stress lasting for centuries. Studies among Red Indians in America, for example, showed drinking habits (and underlying psychological attitudes) not dissimilar to the besieged state of the Irish peasantry in recent centuries.

One could show that the essential psychological attractions of drink, the sense of escapism and hazy well-being, are particularly relevant to a people born and living with a sense of inherited dispossession. One could thus so easily place the burden of moral culpability elsewhere and yet be left with the problem and the overriding evidence that from within the Irish community little effort has been made to contain it. Indeed, membership of the Irish community is to be statistically more prone to becoming part of the problem. As a London conference on Alcoholism was told in 1970: 'In Alcoholics Anonymous they say you don't have to be Irish or Catholic but it gives you a headstart.' The speaker, an Irish social worker (and former alcoholic), declared that 25 per cent of the treatment beds maintained by the Salvation Army in London were occupied by Irish vagrants, yet the total number of such beds attributable to Irish-Catholic agencies was minute: $2\frac{1}{2}$ per cent or in the region of 55 beds as against the Salvation Army's 2,100 in London alone.[6] In other areas of rehabilitation and after-care concern for alcoholics, the proportion of Irish candidates is similarly high, while the Irish share of help is dramatically low. Undoubtedly the disparity is due to the peculiar position of drink in the Irish ethos, and the attendant intricate attitudes towards those who become addicted. Generally, there is a marked reluctance to face the reality of addiction: the word 'alcoholic' being regarded as an impolite noun in many levels of Irish society. Rather there exists a gamut of euphemisms which cushion the medical reality. Phrases such as: 'He has a liking for the hard stuff' are used to describe what is most often a condition of whisky addiction. Or, 'he has a weakness for the drop' may sentimentally cloak the distress of a friend or colleague who cannot see the day through without a substantial intake of alcohol. Indeed addiction sometimes takes on the aura of praise: 'The good man's fault', a commonplace expression, reflects the inherited sexual

[6] The *Guardian*, 19 May 1971.

puritanism of the lower middle-classes: the implication being that indulgence in drink is less culpable than indulgence in sex.

I do not suggest that a heady devotion to Bacchus is the sole prerogative of the Irish—the Scots, French, and Russians have a similar devotion—but rather attempt to express the underlying resistance faced by those involved in rehabilitating the substantial number of Irish alcoholics. That such rescue efforts have met with success is a matter of recorded fact among the many agencies, particularly in London, who deal with alcoholics.

I am grateful to one such agency, the Camberwell Council on Alcoholism, for permission to publish the following case history of rehabilitation of one Irish victim. It does, I think, illustrate not only what is possible in terms of cure, but illuminates also many of the factors which are at the root of 'social problems' among the immigrant Irish.

'IT NEVER SEEMED A PROBLEM TO ME'
An interview with an Irish alcoholic

When did you start drinking?

Regularly from about sixteen.

When did it become a problem to you?

I know now when drink became a problem to me. Years ago I would never go to pubs before first coming home and washing and dressing after work. I would go to the lounge bars on Saturdays and Sundays and meet girls, and think it was a wonderful social life. The downfall started when I began going about with the Irish lads, and working in the building trade, getting £3 a day instead of a regular job. We'd get back from work at six or seven at night, and go into pubs in our working clothes, then the importance of keeping myself tidy seemed to slip away without me knowing it. People began ignoring me, so I stopped going to those pubs. I started going into lower-type pubs, sliding into the East End part of town where everyone was in their working clothes, and where people didn't notice me and accepted me that way. I never noticed myself much either, but the digs kept getting poorer and slummier and the old landladies harder.

I never felt it because I thought I was enjoying myself, and I was that sick the next morning that I couldn't care less where I was. On the days I was sober, I was just working for drink. Then I stopped eating, started saying that a cheese sandwich and a cup of tea is the price of a few pints. I notice these things now, but I never noticed them then. As long as I was getting drink I didn't care.

Eventually I got to the stage where I couldn't keep digs, so I went to Rowton Houses and 'Sallies', but I got barred from them, so I began sleeping out. This was about five years ago. The routine in the last three drinking years in London was to go to the Fish Market at five in the morning and do odd casual jobs, going in and out of the pub till two in the afternoon. Then I'd get two bottles of wine, a bottle of 'jack', and a bottle of cider. When I'd drunk that I'd be drunk the rest of the day. It put me in a sort of delirium, a couldn't-care-less sort of attitude; it didn't make me drunk—it knocked me stupid. I was walking about in a sort of mist.

How frequently have you been arrested for being drunk?

Two or three times a week since I was eighteen.

Did the police ever ask you about your drinking?

Many a time when they took my particulars they'd say, 'This drink's going to kill you. Are you not going to do something about it?'

Have you ever been to prison?

Yes.

Was drinking always the cause?

Every time I was in gaol drink was always in me when I got

caught. I've never done anything criminal in cold-blooded sobriety in my life.

When you were arrested did anyone ever offer you help?

I was never approached, even in prison, no.

From what you know now, when was the first time someone should have said, 'You have a problem. You need help'?

From what I know of alcoholism now, I think if I had got the same chances ten years ago as I got two years ago, I might have been able to do something with them. But was it up to anyone to approach me? I don't know; perhaps I should have had more sense.

What was happening to you ten years ago?

I was living in Birmingham in a single room in the same house with my married brother and sister, and working regularly in the building trade. At that time I would drink from Thursday to Sunday. The rest of the week would be sort of hell, but I always seemed to manage some way.

Did you contact anyone at that time who could have helped you?

I never went officially to see anyone, but I had to go to hospital after I fell off a roof while I was at work.

Were you drunk when you fell?

No, but I was very drunk the night before, so you may guess it was through the effects of drink. I was rushed into casualty with a broken leg and arm and six broken ribs.

Did they go into why you fell off the roof?

No. They asked me what happened and where I lived. It

seemed to me that they were not too keen on letting me stay in hospital.

Why not?

I don't know ... I've never thought about it. I suppose because I was an Irishman and they smelt the fumes of drink off me.

Do you think they could have realized that you had a drinking problem?

I think today they would. There's more being done for alcoholics and more talk about it. But you see, I never had a problem as far as I was concerned. I was living my allotted life, I just accepted it.

When were you first offered help?

Five years ago. A policeman asked me if I was an alcoholic when he found me in a 'skipper' in Bristol. He told me that it was a pity that I had got myself into such a state, as I was only a young man. I said, 'What do you mean? I'm no alcoholic.'

Did he explain what he meant by an alcoholic?

No, but he said there were people you could go to for help. I didn't know what he was talking about, and I wasn't interested at three o'clock in the morning. He gave me a doctor's card and told me to get myself cleaned up when I got paid on Thursday and go down and see the doctor. I didn't do anything about it. I thought an alcoholic was someone who had to drink a bottle of whisky a day. I hadn't heard much talk of them, but when I'd seen them in films they were always rich people.

And you didn't associate them with yourself?

No, you see, everyone I knew was in the same condition as myself and I thought it was the natural thing; I just accepted it

What happened after the policeman spoke to you?

I was very ill so went and stayed at a 'spike' just outside the city from Christmas to March. My nerves were in a terrible state. I never had a drink all that time, though I went to work every day. I was too ill to be bothered with the drink.

Had you made a decision not to drink?

No. I had no intentions of giving up the drink, but it was a very cold winter, and the 'spike' was out in the country. If I'd had any drink in me at all they would have thrown me out. I had got used to the bed, and didn't want to give it up. It was the first time maybe, now that I think about it, that I realized that I had to stay sober for some reason.

Why did you leave?

The money had piled up at the Labour Exchange so I took it and came to London, and then I spent three years knocking about the East End. That was when I first began to get the D.T.s and the shakes really badly.

Did you ever go to hospital?

I was in the casualty department six or seven times, after being hit on the head with bottles and things. They would patch me up and throw me out.

Did they ever do anything more?

Nothing at all. I never saw a social worker or anyone of that kind.

Where did you finally get help?

When I was in the Reception Centre one time, one of the staff asked me to stop in seven days because I was in such a state. Then I saw a doctor there.

How did he help you?

He was marvellous. He deliberately went out of his way to make me angry. I now realize that it was the treatment exactly I needed at the time. We used to nearly come to blows, but at night I couldn't go to sleep for thinking about what he had told me. I didn't always agree with him, but at least he started making me use my mind about myself. Whether I agreed with him or not wasn't the point.

Had you accepted that you were an alcoholic?

Not at first. I was sober in the Centre six weeks and then I went and got drunk for a month before coming back for three months.

Why didn't you go on drinking?

I couldn't. I was feeling really physically ill, worse than when I went in the first time.

Why did you go back to the Centre?

Because of the feeling of conscience I had. It was the first time it really hit me I was throwing away an opportunity. I was drinking with a guilty conscience and feeling that I was deliberately doing something wrong. I wasn't getting any pleasure out of drinking, and for the first time I worried about my condition the next morning. I began realizing that the people at the Centre weren't talking rubbish, and that maybe I *was* an alcoholic. This member of staff at the Centre had really gone out of his way to talk to me; he was the first person who ever took a personal interest in me at all, not only about the drinking, but about everything. He explained a lot about life concerning myself, and I knew he was talking sense. So I went back. The minute he saw me he said he had expected me and that he knew I had something in me, and that I'd come back.

Where did you go from the Centre?

I was on the waiting list to go to a hostel. The doctor called me in one day and said that there was a good hostel nearby and asked me to go to see a psychiatrist about getting in there. The idea of a psychiatrist frightened me; one time when I was in a Centre in the country the warden threatened that he would have me certified by a psychiatrist. But I went to the hospital to see this one about the hostel and I liked him from the moment I saw him. He was very quiet and didn't ask me many questions. Then he asked me if I would be willing to let him try to help me. I agreed, and went into the hostel the following week.

How did you get on in the hostel?

The Group Therapy meetings kept me on my mettle. I was a rebel right from the beginning, but if you go into these hostels to be a model pupil, they can't help you. You've got to be honest with yourself and sincere, and not worry about sounding nice and agreeable at the meetings. I was also helped while I was there by friends I made outside; they weren't alcoholics. I met them through going to help voluntarily the different organizations that give aid to drinking alcoholics and homeless men in general. They gave me a lot of encouragement and personal interest and would explain and help me with things that came up at meetings.

How long have you been sober now?

Two years.

And why do you remain sober?

When I was drinking, before I went to the Reception Centre, I was in complete ignorance. I lost everything by degrees and I never missed it going. I never sat down and looked at what I missed through drinking. It never seemed a problem to me. I couldn't slip into that state again—I've learnt so much in the last two years. I couldn't unconsciously throw away my life the way I did before. There would be no innocence behind it if I drank again.

There are many clues in that interview which highlight factors relevant to the entire ethos of Irish immigration. It may be noted that the subject began to go downhill when he became 'involved with the Irish lads and working in the building trade'.

The observation occurs that he found some more fulfilling measure of identity there, among those who, bereft of other social alternatives, make the pub their social centre of warmth and cameraderie.

'It seemed to me they were not too keen on letting me stay in hospital ... because I was an Irishman and they smelt the fumes of drink.' A classic example of the sense of alienation felt by many immigrants, an alienation most comfortably cloaked in spurious comradeship of the pub. Further, the subject registered the feeling, exaggerated most often among groups of Irish building workers, of unspoken hostility on the dual grounds of dress and nationality. 'I was in the casualty department six or seven times, after being hit on the head ... they would patch me up and throw me out.'

'Just another drunken Paddie' may well have been the reaction of an overworked hospital staff. Someone else, however, had a more humane view: '[the doctor] was marvellous ... We used to nearly come to blows but at night I couldn't go to sleep for thinking about what he had told me ... *he was the first person who ever took an interest in me at all* ... He explained a lot about life concerning myself, and I knew he was talking sense.'

There are, one feels, many pointers in that interview which may account for the excessive numbers of Irish in Britain who form that sub-group of afflicted flotsam. It is a telling commentary upon the self-lauded claims of 'Christian Ireland' that every year a proportion of her emigrants to Britain will—by that first step aboard the emigrant boat—also head for the loneliness and humiliation of the alcoholically afflicted. Whatever the personality factors during their time in Ireland which predispose them to become addicts in Britain, the fact is that concerned, professional help from among the Irish community in Britain is almost non-existent; an area of neglect in stark contrast to some other achievements of self-help. Given that record of self-help, particularly during the past decade, it may be reasonable to assume that in time similar inroads will be made upon this area of human need.

The Settled Community

The 'community' feeling among the million Irish-born who reside, for the most part, permanently in Britain is a comparatively recent development and certainly within the confines of the last decade. They had, hitherto, been regarded as a community more by their hosts than by themselves, and even now tended to be regarded, as former Labour Government Minister Roy Hattersley wrote in *The Times* in February 1971, '... as all the same. To their detractors they appear uniformly violent and unskilled, with a pick-axe in one hand, a bottle of stout in the other and the name of a building contractor stencilled on their backs. Even their champions often mount no more persuasive a defence than our duty to be grateful for the railways, canals, and roads that could not have been built without them. Ireland's disproportionately large contribution to the British Army's General Staff is usually overlooked.'

It is not, of course, only to the General Staff of the British Army that the present Irish presence is to be noted, but more characteristically among the 10,000 Irish-born who form around 6 per cent of the 172,000-strong land forces. And thought the Irish navvies still predominate on the building sites, the 'name of a building contractor stencilled upon their backs' is increasingly likely to be an Irish one. And while popular reaction may see as typically Irish the boozy antics of a drunk on a late-night train, the policeman who books the drunk into a cell for the night might well be as Irish. Residual images, however, persist. As reported in an issue of the Birmingham *Evening Mail* of November 1965, the then Lord Mayor, Mr Corbyn-Barrow, noted: 'If you look at the list of persons for trial at the Quarter Sessions, you will realize what difficulties there are in assimilating the Irish into the life of the city. As you look down the list, you will see it is almost entirely Irish names.'

His remarks, by no means unusual at the time, reflected an image of the Irish which, however validly based, sounded echoes of unease among the growing segment of middle-class and 'voluntary' immigrants of recent years, and among those of previous generations who in the sixties had evolved to a sense of fruitful adjustment to their lives in Britain. From mixed motives of self-interest—'to upgrade the image' and social responsibility—'let's help our less fortunate'—there evolved some sense of community awareness, characterized by the activities of the Federation of Irish Societies. Founded in Portsmouth in 1964 by, perhaps predictably, three Corkmen (of professional occupation), the Federation subsequently provided the embryo structure wherein the various, and previously disparate, Irish organizations may cohesively contribute towards community self-help, notably in the expansion of Irish centres and the attendant growth of welfare facilities. In this regard, the Federation was instrumental in securing substantial financial loans from the Bass Charrington Brewery towards the purchase of premises for centres and in 1972 the Federation sponsored a conference of delegates from forty Irish societies to formulate a cohesive approach to welfare and 'social problems', an indication of the growing sense of independence, and reality, towards the permanence of the Irish community in Britain.

This sense of permanence, however, raises questions of identity and attitude. How Irish are the Irish in Britain?

It is a question not easily answered, for the only immediate comparison can be with the Irish in Ireland who themselves reflect many diverse traits, and in some respects a minority of the settled Irish in Britain appear more Irish than the Irish in Ireland. At many Irish clubs, for instance, the playing of the Irish National Anthem is attended with more respect than at any similar gathering in Ireland (except in the Catholic areas of Ulster). Similarly the surfeit of shamrocks, tricolours, and patriot portraits which adorn most Irish clubs in Britain would appear incongruous and dated in establishments in the Republic. Likewise, the degree of enthusiasm displayed by parents in having their children avail of Irish dancing classes, for which there is an extensive waiting list, appears almost excessive to casual visitors from Ireland. For such supporters of things Irish in Britain there is little self-doubt as to their sense of identity, although it may appear to the outside observer that such devotion to cultural insignia reflects an unwillingness to adjust to the more cosmopolitan possibilities of their new environment.

Certainly the gamut of institutional symbols is wide-ranging, from regular attendance at Sunday Mass and the weekly purchase of newspapers from Ireland, to the unfailing trip home every year, all of which serve as reassurance of identity and which may superficially appear to offer evidence of unsettlement in Britain, but which on reflection may be more accurately judged as the compensatory needs of those who have, in fact, settled. Accordingly, some contact with things Irish serves as a reminder of another country, to which the émigré Irish for the most part are unlikely to return to permanent habitation. For in spite of their green-tinted praise of the virtues of Ireland, immigrants display a marked reluctance to return home in any meaningful numbers. 'The Banks of My Own Lovely Lee,' as Dominic Behan has remarked, are especially lovely to Corkmen on a Saturday night in Kilburn—happily two hundred miles away from the self-same banks.

They remain, nevertheless, Irish in many aspects of temperament; in their (for the most part) adherence to Catholicism, in their suspicion of 'pagan' values, and in their hard-headed awareness of economic reality. When the *Irish Post* asked of its readers: 'Given an equivalent income, would you return to live permanently in Ireland?' 85 per cent answered yes, yet nowhere near that proportion have in fact returned in recent years, in spite of the greatly improved economic situation in the sixties which would have provided many returned emigrants with an equivalent income in real terms.

Why then have not more returned? The answer is almost totally economic, involving many complicated factors. A random questioning conducted by this writer among Irish-born showed that while the most widespread single response was a straight economic one: 'better pay and living conditions', other economically-influential factors were almost as weighty, including a distrust of the Irish economy and, among the middle-aged, a residual memory of 'hard times' in Ireland. In the case of parents, a potent reason was a marked reluctance to uproot their children from what they regarded as being educational opportunities and future career prospects in Britain.

Outside of economic considerations, some respondents simply felt that they were happier in Britain than in Ireland, and enjoyed the stimulation of cosmopolitan life, in particular the forging of friendships with non-Irish people, while the longer-settled displayed some unease at the real or imagined problems of re-settling in Ireland. More than half, however, said they would return to Ireland 'sometime', an answer which betrays some measure of self-deception; as mentioned earlier, available figures indicate a much lesser number returning to permanent habitation in recent years. Nevertheless, almost all regarded themselves as Irish and could not foresee themselves formally adopting British nationality, while a minority displayed signs of trenchant Irishness in the sense of frequenting Irish clubs, regularly reading the *Irish Post* and reacting strongly to what they see as evidence of stock English attitudes towards them.

Observer journalist Patrick O'Donovan has written of 'the predictable flood of letters to the editor whenever anything remotely controversial is written about religion or Ireland. These are formidable letters and the most daunting come from Irish Catholics who live in England and who, like pain-maddened buffaloes, attack on sight. And they savage you, not only for what you said, but for not saying what they think you ought to have said. I sometimes feel that this particular sort of exile is activated by unconscious guilt about not being in Ireland.'

Whatever the likely truth of that last assertion—and it may indeed explain the excessive Irishness of a minority—the prickly sensitivity can be potent, as the *Irish Post* painfully discovered. Some months after the paper was launched (with a green-inked masthead and the slogan: 'The Voice of the Irish in Britain') it published a front-page story headed 'Sex Goes Underground' which recited, half tongue-in-cheek, the plans of a well-known London-Irish publican and publicist, Buttie Sugrue, to bury underground a man and wife until such time as the wife conceived. Reaction from outraged members of the community was swift; the paper was promptly banned from sale outside many North London Catholic churches and the flow of abusive letters and telephone calls continued for some weeks. It was a curious phenomenon of sensitivity provoked more by the impression possibly given to non-Irish readers, rather than to any integral bad taste of the story itself, a classic reaction of 'what will the neighbours say?' (neighbours in this case being the British at large) and one which betokened a sense of insecure settlement. One indignant woman reader charged that 'it's the sort of story one expects to find in *The People* newspaper . . .' and when taxed she admitted that *The People* was read regularly in her home, but that 'we expect better from an Irish paper, especially a paper about the Irish in England'. It is the most obviously 'Irish' (including some with English accents) of the immigrants who generally display the strongest reaction to real or imagined slurs and who can hardly be strictly divided among class terms, but reflects rather the personal sense of security or adjustment of individuals. Predictably, the longer-settled tend to ignore, or even no longer notice, what the newcomer may be highly sensitive to; the Irish, after all, have been prominent as the butt of humour in the British consciousness for at least the past century, and it is entirely reasonable that most native-born British, when confronted with an Irish situation, should react from that inherited imagery of the Irish.

It may be relevant, nonetheless, to note the extent to which these automatic attitudes towards the Irish still persist. When thirty hours of video tape of the highly successful 1971 television series, 'The Comedians', was analysed it was found that: 'the jokes the comedians told in order of frequency were: 1. Anti-Pakistani, 2. Anti-Irish, 3. Anti-Semitic, 4. Anti-docker, 5. Sexual'.[1] On television the Irish drunk, villain, or priest is almost a routine encounter in any one week's viewing, but a more revealing insight into unconscious attitudes was provided by writer Christopher Logue (admittedly Jesuit-educated and of Irish descent) when he translated a play of the Belgian writer Hugo Claus for production at London's Royal Court Theatre in November 1971. *The Times* reviewer,

[1] *Sunday Times*, 5 December 1971.

having outlined the play which has incest as one of its themes, noted that 'it is hard ... to know how to divide credit between the Belgian author and his translator, Christopher Logue ... when the truth comes out about George's incest, what would be the Belgian equivalent of the reaction: "It's common enough among the Irish; but as for you, George, a rate-payer ..."?'

Undoubtedly the native attitudes expressed by the media affect the sense of Irishness among the immigrants, producing among the devotees a trenchant reinforcement of their nationality and perhaps contributing among the greater diffused proportion a conscious diluting of such obvious Irish characteristics as accent and turn of phrase. For it is among the greater proportion who do not frequent Irish clubs or surround themselves with the props of spurious identity that the true conflicts of identity occur; among those who have found their emigration rewarding, succeeding at their work and having valued friendships among the English; those who, in Conor Cruise O'Brien's phrase 'most experience their duality', that the pressures to transfer cultural and political loyalties are most severe. Said Roy Hattersley: '... the Irish are only totally accepted in British society when they lose their Irish characteristics. If their accent is obvious and if their children—being Catholic—do not attend the local school, there is the underlying suspicion that sooner or later they will come home blind drunk. The assumption is nonsense. But it is nevertheless dangerous, particularly so for Irishmen who want a mortgage, promotion or public office.'

The assumption was felt by the increasing number of middle-class Irish in the sixties who came in pursuit of mortgage and promotion—if not public office—and provided momentum for many to divest themselves, in so far as they could, of Irish extremities of accent or behaviour, leading, in some cases, to comical hybrids whose broad vowel sounds keep breaking through adopted genteel tones.

Such hybrids are, however, tiny in number; most of the 'middle-class' Irish in Britain are almost indistinguishable from their counterparts in Ireland, except perhaps in areas where, in this writer's experience, they tend to be more liberal in attitudes of sexual morality and less hidebound by anti-British feeling than the same class in Ireland. They are also, given the competitive nature of British metropolitan life, more industrious, have fewer children, and may be marginally wealthier; and, if the desire was sufficiently strong, could make the transfer back to Ireland with greater ease than, say, the mass of working-class Irish labour.

Accordingly, they may in many respects not feel the need to assert their Irishness here, preferring gently to absorb, and be absorbed into, the rituals of middle-class and upper middle-class English life which many find agreeable and stimulating. There is much written about the 'charm of the Irish', a much more potent force may be the 'charm of the English' and particularly the lure of certain English rituals of life-style which project an almost irresistible aura for many post-imperial Irish. It is no accident that the B.B.C. receives an inordinately large number of applications from Irishmen; that the various branches of the former Colonial Service were heavily staffed with Irish; that the Limerick-born actor Richard Harris was regarded as having brought off some sort of coup in marrying a Lord's daughter; or that the Right-Wing Monday Club, sometimes referred to as 'the conscience of Conservatives', contains some Irish-born members.

Even for the Irish in Ireland, influences arising from the proximity of Britain are widespread; tastes in clothes, reading matter, and general life-style invariably follow—often after a ten-year interval—those of Britain, so that most emigrants to the larger island are already conditioned in many respects for absorption in their social stream in Britain. It is an absorption which, given the settlement of the Ulster issue, is likely to apply to the majority of immigrants, particularly when accompanied by material success and the forging of satisfactory careers. One successful architect, the beneficiary of such advances, gave his attitude as: 'being very reluctant to return to Ireland. Apart from the risk of lowering my standard of living, in other areas my life is better here; I have more trustworthy friends, and though it gives me no particular pleasure to say so, I regard their attitude towards me as being more Christian than many in Ireland', a reaction echoed by some who do return and find in journalist Mary Kenny's phrase, that 'while the Irish may give a welcome to strangers, they are not, in my experience, notably hospitable to returned emigrants. An element of suspicion attaches to those who return, with their moral attitudes in particular being scrutinized for evidence of pollution by the notions prevailing abroad.'

After a few years' trail-blazing journalistic work in Ireland Mary Kenny returned to London because 'being a career girl I couldn't resist the challenge of the job I was offered as features editor of the *Evening Standard*' (she is one of the few women to hold such a position in Fleet Street) and also because 'Ireland can be intellectually stifling; you meet the same people over and over again and have the same conversations repetitively. London is more mind-expanding, and from an intellectual point of view, it challenges you more.'

A comparable reaction, put by a twenty-three-year-old girl from a city in provincial Ireland, was that: 'I had to get out, or burst. I couldn't take the heavy moral "respectability"; to be frank, I couldn't express myself sexually; I was afraid that if I stayed I would have ended up marrying some fellow I went out with for a few years and spend the rest of my life wondering what I might have missed. So all in a week I decided, drew fifty pounds out of the bank, which I blew in two weeks of sightseeing in London.' After that she took a flat in Bayswater, a well-paid job, being a trained commercial artist, and a lover. She vaguely holds the idea of returning home, but 'not for some years yet. There's too much excitement for me here, finding out about myself in the context of other people.'

She exemplifies the growing proportion of 'voluntary emigrants' of recent years who come for a variety of reasons other than economic, and who bring with them no profound sense of Irishness. But even among the bulk of semi-skilled and labouring immigrants, the strong sense of Irishness is confined to a minority and it is from this minority that the continuum of racial awareness is transmitted through the generations. A pointer to this degree of Irishness was revealed in a survey carried out at a North London Catholic School in 1970, among 100 school children of Irish parentage, of whom 52 per cent regarded themselves as *neither* exclusively English or Irish, but 'a mixture of both', with the remaining 48 per cent dividing equally into English and Irish identifications of nationality. The figure of 62 per cent who had never attended any specific Irish club or function confirms the impression that a smaller proportion of immigrants participate in any outward declarations of Irishness, but in contrast (and perhaps in keeping with general emotional attachments) over half said they would cheer for Ireland in a football match against England.[2] This tenuous, if sporting, link with the land of their parents would seem to corroborate, and characterize the attitude of the majority of settled Irish, who for the most part would not wish their children to grow up with any stultifying extremity of Irishness, a view confirmed by the teacher who conducted the survey when he commented: 'Considering that most of the children have so far lived their lives in Britain, it is right that they should regard themselves as British; to go on regarding themselves as outsiders would only lead to future discontent and unhappiness.'

A more extreme report on being brought up in a strongly Irish—and Catholic—atmosphere in Britain was provided by writer John O'Callaghan.

To be brought up as an Irish Catholic in England is to be nurtured as a schizophrenic. I received an English education which may, I forget, have managed to include a sentence somewhere about the 1845 famine. History is the most obvious place to see first the effect of being introduced to a background of which I was not the true inheritor. In the flux of post-war schooling, class distinctions remained clear with public, grammar, and secondary modern schools giving appropriate training to the country's money, brains, and muscle.

Immigrant parents can be very isolated. Loving the material comforts, they lack the right social reflexes. So they —in my case—gave thanks for the blessings of escaping the milking stool in Clare by endorsing all the values of Clare. Sunday mass, serving one week-day mass, benedic-

[2] *Irish Post*, 23 December 1970.

tion, family rosary, these mechanisms of religious certainty were automatic. I was a kind of religious athlete in good trim.

Catholicism makes for one set of differences, while being Irish makes for another set; Irish people explode quicker, shout louder, sulk sooner than English. It was not until the sixth form that Irishness gained a status. And then it was the status of the acceptable Irish traits of humour, gab, directness and not the sad attributes of peevishness, deceit, and intractability. About this stage the brighter specimens recognized the shape of society, realized they would not come into its promised land as Irish creations. They honed up their accents, and bought a regimental tie.

But the Irish—the native Irish—presence of my parents at home brought reminders that the fair play, the self control, the impartiality of the British is as skin deep as in any other race. Hearsay at home of the Black and Tans, the Famine, Cromwell, shows the son of immigrants very early that things in England are not always what they seem. You are born outside furrows of thought that some pure natives never see over. It is worth risking the schizophrenia to be reared without blinkers.

'Risking the schizophrenia' may well characterize the endeavour of the Irish in Britain who, in spite of their increased cohesion, remain something of a neutered people, free of the full vigour of British life on the one hand, and of Irish life on the other.

Of Ireland, yet no longer living there. Of Britain now, yet not feeling British; geographically cut-off from the mainspring of their own native culture without being easily adaptable to the alternative one. They are nevertheless destined, however strident their protests, to be absorbed into the melting-pot of a multi-racial society. From whence, like the generations before them, the bones of their names will emerge in some future Labour cabinet, in trade unions, in the professions, and in every aspect of life in Britain.

PART III

Appendix

'Being Irish is a state of mind,' wrote *Observer* journalist Patrick O'Donovan, born in Britain of an Irish doctor and M.P. Apart from temperamental inclinations, however, the legal definition of Irish rests with a multiplicity of enactments of the British and Irish Parliaments. The main source of recognition probably rests with the Irish Nationality and Citizenship Act of Dail Eireann of 1956, which specifies that:

Any person born in any part of Ireland is Irish and continues to be Irish, irrespective of where they live. The only exception to this is somebody who has formally taken nationality in another country.

Any person born in Northern Ireland after 1922 whose parents or grandparents were born anywhere in Ireland is Irish in the same manner as already specified.

Any person born in Northern Ireland after 1922 whose parents or grandparents were not born in Ireland may declare themselves Irish and have an Irish passport. Such people must sign an informal declaration giving details of date and place of birth and of current residence.

Anyone born in Britain, or elsewhere, of Irish parents or grandparents is entitled to Irish citizenship and an Irish passport on request.

The Irish constitution recognizes an individual's right to dual-nationality—although two passports may not be held at the one time.

HOW MANY PERSONS OF IMMEDIATE IRISH DESCENT IN BRITAIN?

It is difficult to compute a precise figure, but conservatively estimated at around four million, the principal pointer to this estimate being the figure of six million nominal members of the Roman Catholic religion in Britain, of which at least half may be reasonably held to be of immediate (first to third generation) Irish extraction. Bearing in mind the 'leakage' away from Roman Catholicism of a proportion of immigrants, and the fact that a minority are not, and were not, Catholics, plus the high fertility rate of Irish marriages (70 per cent above national average in 1966), the figure of *four million* Britons of Irish extraction may be taken as a reasonable approximation.

HOW MANY IRISH-BORN IN BRITAIN?

Over one million in round figures, or approximately 2 per cent of the population of Great Britain. The last available census figure, for 1966, declares a figure of 948,320 Irish-born in England, Wales, and Scotland. It is accepted by census officials that this figure may underestimate the true number, not least in the proportion of Irish-born who, for a variety of personal and financial reasons, are likely to have absented themselves during the visits of census enumerators. In the 'Population Census' by Bernard Benjamin, the author shows that a check survey held after the 1961 census revealed that the question of nationality was not answered by 'a significant proportion'. Thus a conservative estimate places the number of Irish-born at over one million.

WHERE DO THEY COME FROM IN IRELAND?

1966 Census:	from Irish Republic:	713,170
	from Northern Ireland:	209,530
	part of Ireland not stated:	25,620
		948,320

FROM WHAT REGIONS IN IRELAND?

Of the four provinces of Ireland—Leinster, Munster, Connacht, and Ulster—the western province of Connacht provides the highest proportion of immigrants to Britain. In the period 1966–71, for example, Connacht lost 10·6 persons per 1,000 of population, by contrast with the more industrialized eastern province of Leinster, which lost only 2·2 per 1,000. In the immediate post-Famine migrations of a century ago, the province of Munster lost the most people, with the highest number leaving the county of Cork. Today, the county of Leitrim in Connacht is the chief sufferer through emigration.

WHERE DO THEY SETTLE IN BRITAIN?

Principally in urban areas; in the principal towns Irish-born constitute approximately one in forty of the population.

HOW DO THEY COMPARE IN SOCIO-ECONOMIC STATUS TO THE NATIVE POPULATION?

Abstracts from the 1966 Census show that, among samples of economically-active males, the contrast was:

	Born in Ireland	Born in England and Wales
Professional workers	1·0%	3·1%
Employers and Managers	3·6%	8·3%
Non-Manual	13·2%	22·1%
Skilled Manual	36·5%	39·6%
Semi-skilled Manual	19·7%	15·7%
Unskilled Manual	24·8%	9·9%

HOW DO THE IRISH-BORN COMPARE WITH COLOURED (COMMONWEALTH) IMMIGRANTS?

Both immigrant groups are almost equal in numbers at around one million each. The Irish generally follow better-paid occupations than coloured immigrants, live in better housing conditions, and on average have more children per family at 2·52 children, as against an average of 2·24 children for coloured immigrant families.

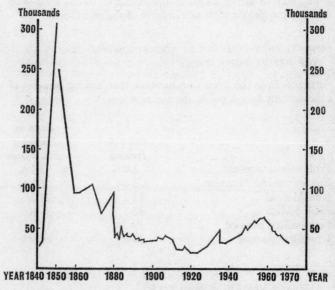

THE PATTERN OF IRISH EMIGRATION TO BRITAIN
FROM 1840 TO THE PRESENT DAY

One notable difference is that of sex-composition; unlike coloured immigrant groups where men predominate over women, the Irish hold a ratio of 912 males to every 1,000 females.

Comparing the three communities of Irish, coloured, and native British, available abstracts from the 1961 and 1966 Census suggest that: (1) the Irish approximate most to the native British community in areas of employment, housing, and education. (2) The Irish are most like the coloured community in areas of family size. (3) In areas of 'social problems', i.e. criminal offences, the Irish have a higher proportion than either native or coloured communities.

HOW THE IRISH CAME—AND STILL COME—TO BRITAIN

The general trend of Irish emigration to Britain, computed from various sources.* Allowing for margins of error in individual years, due to inadequate or conflicting records, this graph nevertheless records the general trend of the Irish diaspora to Britain since the Great Famine of 1845–7.

Although the Irish had come to Britain since earliest times, the successive famines of the early 1800s gave impetus to the tradition, culminating in the exodus from the Great Famine of 1845–7. During that period, and in the years immediately following, upwards of a quarter of a million a year came to Britain; around half of that number subsequently went to further destinations overseas, mainly America and Australia.

* Returns of the Irish Registrar-General, British Census, British Home Office figures on Insurance and Social Welfare cards since 1948, *Commission on Emigration*, Dublin, 1954.

Bibliography

The following works were consulted:

George Andrew Beck, ed., *The English Catholics 1850–1950*, London: Burns, Oates, 1950.

Brendan Behan, *Borstal Boy*, London: Hutchinson, 1958.

Brian Behan, *With Breast Expanded* (with a dedication to 'money and flat-chested women'), London: MacGibbon & Kee, 1964.

Maire Brock, 'Irish Immigrants in Manchester, 1830–54', unpublished thesis, University of Southampton, 1962.

Mary Cathcart Borer, *Liverpool*, London: Longman, 1970.

David Butler and Michael Pinto-Duschinsky, *The British General Election, 1970*, London: Macmillan, 1971.

Winston Churchill, *The Second World War*, 6 vols. London: Educational Book Co., 1946–8.

R. Clayton, ed., *Geography of Greater London*, London: George Philip, 1964.

Terry Coleman, *The Railway Navvies*, London: Hutchinson, 1965 (Pelican paperback ed., 1968).

Tim Pat Coogan, *The I.R.A.*, London: Pall Mall Press, 1970 (Fontana paperback ed., 1971).

Margery Forester, *Michael Collins*, London: Sidgwick & Jackson, 1970.

James E. Handley, *The Irish in Modern Scotland*, Cork University Press, 1947.

—— *The Irish in Scotland*, Cork University Press, 1943.

John Archer Jackson, *The Irish in Britain*, London: Routledge & Kegan Paul, 1964.

Patrick Kavanagh, *The Green Fool*, London: Martin Brian & O'Keeffe, 1971.

Donall MacAmhlaigh, *An Irish Navvy*, London: Routledge & Kegan Paul, 1964.

Shelley Markham, *What About the Irish?* London: Runnymede Trust (Information Paper), 1971.

Henry Mayhew, *London Labour and the London Poor*, London: Griffin, Bohn & Co., 1861.

Drew Middleton, *The British*, London: Secker & Warburg, 1957.

Millicent Rose, *The East End of London*, London: Cresset Press, 1951.

George Scott, *The R.C.'s*, London: Hutchinson, 1964.

Graham Turner, *An Economic History of Britain*, London: Eyre & Spottiswoode, 1966.

Bernard Ward, *Catholic Emancipation 1829–1929*, London: Longman, 1929.

—— *Catholic London a Century Ago*, London: The Catholic Truth Society, 1905.

Commission on Emigration and other Population Problems, 1948–54, Dublin: Stationery Office, 1954.

Various pamphlets and Annual Reports of the Irish Centre, Camden Town (during the sixties), and of the Anti-Partition League (during the fifties).

Various journals, periodicals, and British and Irish newspapers.

Index